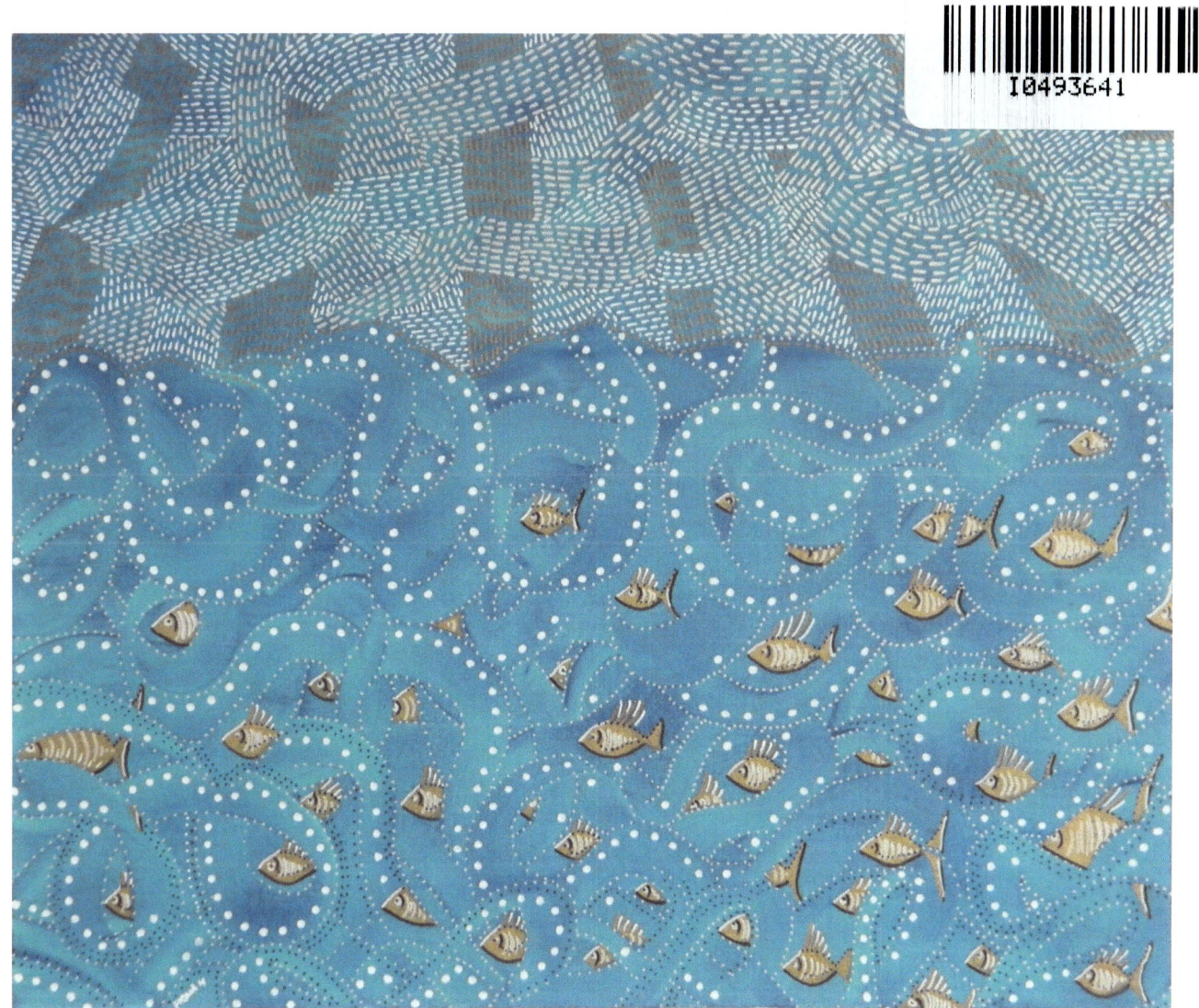

Steam punk fish by Fionna Henderson

Front cover:
Evening sail by Geoff Lewis

Introduction

I was first introduced to the world of art by a very inspirational art teacher at High School. I think that since leaving school I have probably read every book on the subject of painting, and with trial and error over a long period of time I have learnt my craft. I have not allowed myself to be tied to one subject or style of painting and always enjoy the challenge of trying something new.

I have been asked on many occasions if I would teach painting with acrylic, I hear many stories from people with all sorts of reasons why they have not tried painting with acrylic paint. Well there is no excuse, with a bit of perseverance you can do anything. This book is aimed at you whether beginner or practised artist in other mediums .

Enjoyment is key, no matter what you aspire to achieve with your art. I always advocate that playing gets results, we all learned as children through play, so why not as adults? The purpose of this book is to allow you to play with the techniques discussed in this book.

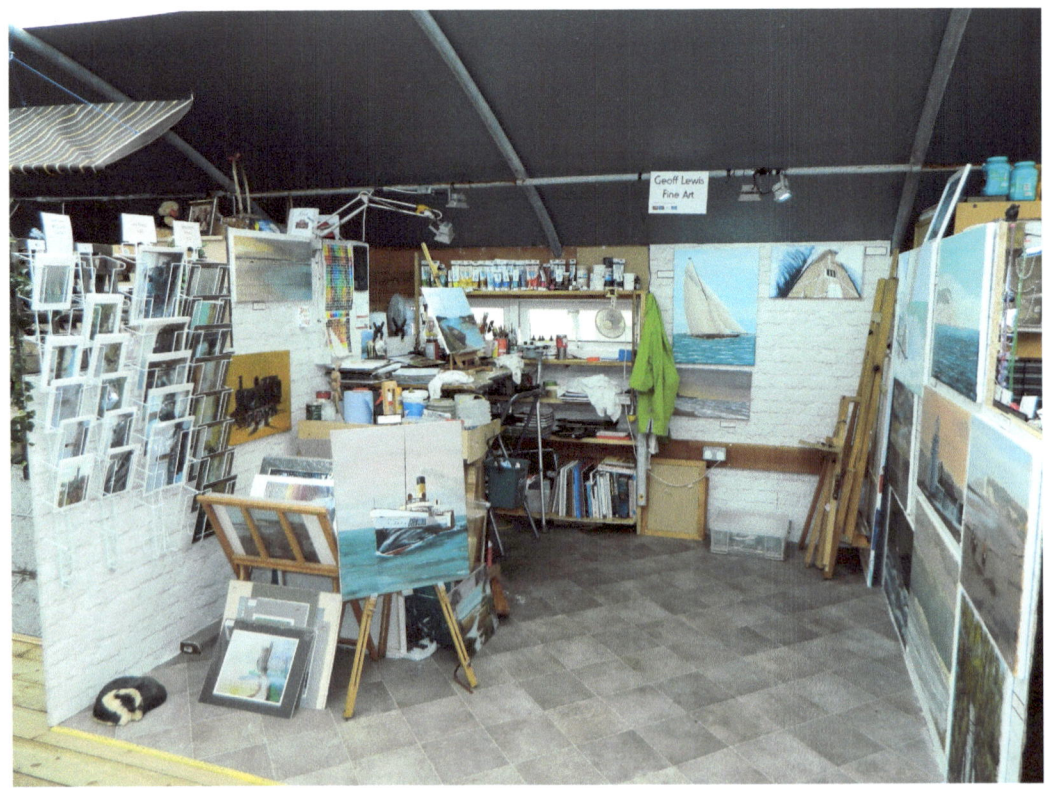

Geoff Lewis is a self taught artist who lives and works on the Isle of Wight.
His studio is located at Island Studios, Holliers Park, close to Sandown and is open daily.

www.big-geoff.co.uk

Index

Acrylic paint. How is it made.

Acrylic paint is the product of the plastics industry, originally designed for the automotive industry and very quickly taken up by artists as an alternative to oils. The binder that holds the pigment is a polymer resin that once dry gives hard, clear plastic coating. Being plastic it is pliable and won't crack, and cannot be removed.

The pigments are the same natural pigments as used in oils and watercolour with some being made in the laboratory such as Alizarin crimson, Naphthalene Lemon.

Pros and cons

Acrylic paint is very versatile; there are no rules as to how you can use it. It can be laid down thick or thin or used as watercolours. In the early days of using acrylic there was an issue over the paint drying too quickly and is often quoted as a reason not to use it. There are now a large range of additives and mediums available, with slow drying mediums especially made to alleviate the issue of drying time.

Additives

Lets talk about the different additives available to use with acrylic paints.

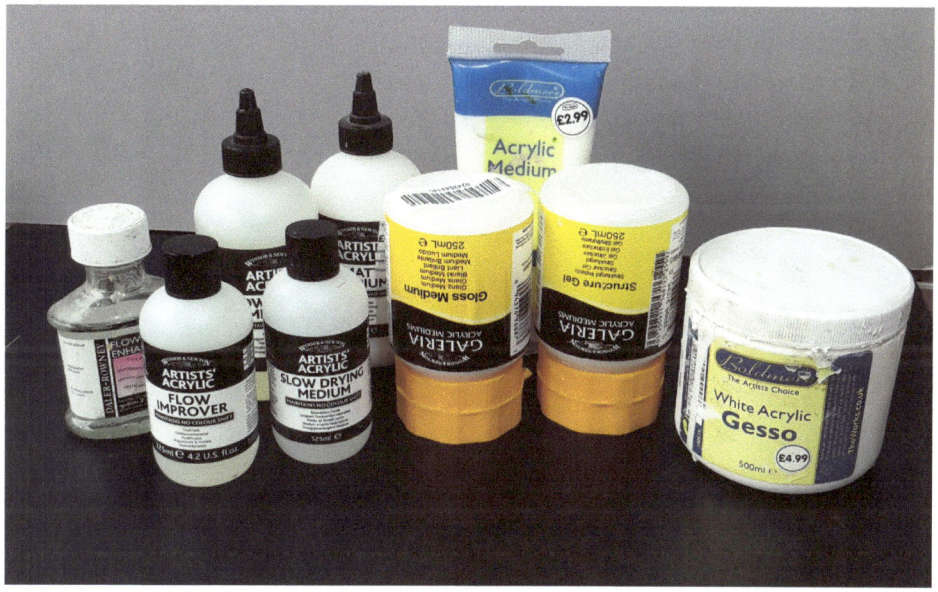

I have mentioned slow drying medium and its ability to keep paint wet longer which helps with blending colours on the canvas.

There are Flow Improver's/Enhancer's which breaks the bonds in the water to give a much more efficient flow of the paint, ideal for painting large flat surfaces, or fine detail where you want the paint to flow evenly.

Gloss and Matt mediums give body to the paint without losing the vibrancy of the colour they also extend the drying time of the paint and are good wet on wet painting.

Glazing medium is used for making glazes of transparent colour, it dries clear letting the colour beneath show through. It is used for skies, seas, water or anywhere you want to add luminosity to your paintings. You can use the same glazing techniques as in oils, because of the quick drying time they are much easier in Acrylic than in Oils.

Structure Gels give body to paints for impasto technique without the need for buying heavy body paints.

Other additives include glass beads, sands, stringing gel for adding texture to your Paintings.

Tools

There is a vast range of tools available to the artist, I have collected quite a range of brushes, Pallet Knives, sponges and scrapers. You don't need to spend a great deal to start painting.

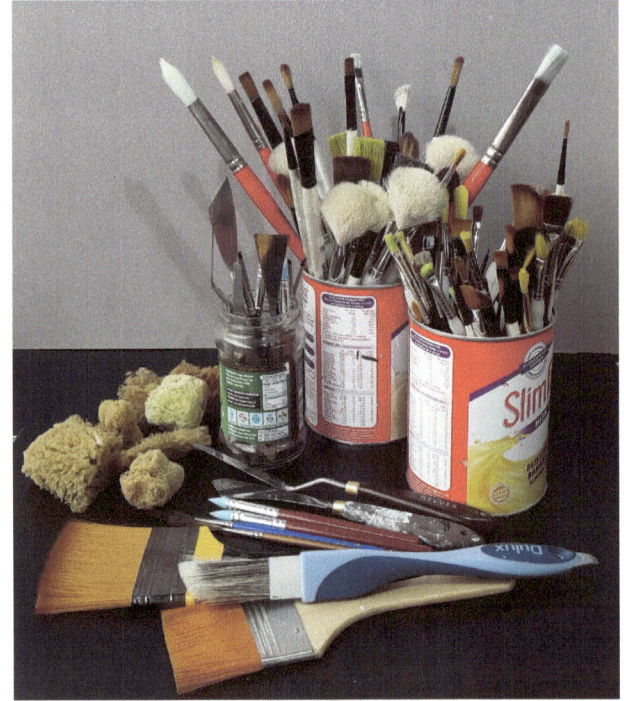

I use Nylon brushes from my local art store that are reasonably priced and they are of a good quality; I always recommend when purchasing brushes to buy locally as you can see what you are buying and can feel the texture and firmness of the bristles.

Pallet or Painting Knives are made with flexible steel or plastic they are relatively inexpensive and essential for mixing paint on your pallet and for painting with.

Scrapers can be purchased from your local art shop or you can make your own.

For large surfaces there are wide brushes but as an alternative you can use good quality household brushes.

You can water down acrylic paint to apply with an Airbrush, although you should thoroughly clean the equipment after each use.

Hair dryer? I use one to get washes quickly dry before adding more paint, not an essential tool but I find it useful for when I want to work quickly.

Brushes

Don't spend large amounts of money on expensive brushes to start with. Look for Daler Rowney Graduate series or Winsor & Newton University series or Royal Soft grip brushes. These can be purchased relatively cheaply from your local art shop.

When purchasing brushes it is always good to handle the brushes before you purchase them as you can asses the spring, softness and quality of the brush.

Recommended brushes.
3/4" Flat, 1/2" Flat,
#3, 4, & 6 Round, #2 Rigger
1/2" & #10 Filberts.

These brushes will be enough to get you started, although you may want to add a 2" flat brush for larger areas of colour.

Pallet & Painting Knives

You can get these in a cheap plastic but I would advise caution using these. Try and get the steel knives as these are much more flexible, again ask in your local art shop they are relatively cheap to purchase. I would recommend 2 painting knives and 1 pallet knife.

Mixing Pallet

There are many types and shapes and sizes available, try and get the largest one you can as you will need a large area for mixing your colours on.

Mediums and Additives

Winsor & Newton produce a good range of mediums, you will need a Matt Medium and a Slow Drying Medium.

As you start experimenting you will pick up other tools and materials to use, always ask your local art shop for help in what you need. They have a wealth of experience and knowledge and are always helpful.

Grounds

Acrylic paint is also very versatile with application to surfaces. The usual surface being canvas, it can also be used on MDF, ply wood, pardboard, concrete, brickwork, metal, glass the list goes on and on. As long as there is a tooth for the paint to adhere to you can paint on it. When painting on a porous surface be sure to seal the surface with a primer and several coats of Gesso, a mixture of Acrylic primer and colour. This can be lightly sanded to give a smooth painting surface.

Paints

If you are just starting out I recommend that you look at purchasing a starter set of acrylic paints, It is best if you can get a set of 10 colours as you will have enough colours to produce a large range of colour mixes.

The range of producers of acrylic paints is fairly large, you can get student paint at very reasonable prices right up to the highest quality professional paints.

Colours

There are literally hundreds of paint colours available across a very wide range of manufacturers. Try not to get the cheapest paint as you will not get the quality of pigmentation you require.

The paints I have chosen to use are from Daler-Rowney as they offer a range of colours that can be relatively inexpensive but have very good quality pigments, which is to me very important.

They also produce their range in heavy body medium which are good for impasto work. If I need a more exotic colours I go for A2 Chroma paints, another heavy body paint with very good quality pigments. Be aware that some of the more exotic colours can be expensive depending on the manufacturer.

Always try and get the best quality paints that you can afford, but don't go mad spending a lot on every colour available. Look to have between 3 to 4 colours of each colour group and make sure you have secondary and intermediary colours not all primary colours (See colour theory for more information).

I have about 50 individual colours to hand, these are not all used at the same time some rarely and depending upon the subject material, I may have about 6 to 10 on my pallet for an individual painting.

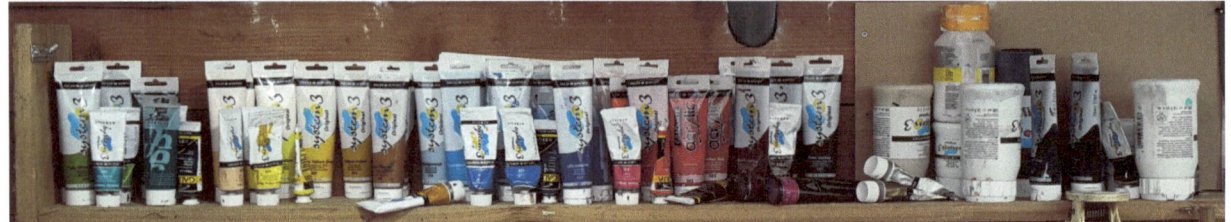

Some of the paints in my studio

My most used colours are:

Yellows and Browns

Pale olive Green, Cadmium Yellow, Yellow Ochre, Raw Sienna, Burnt Sienna, Burnt Umber and Raw Umber

Blues

Wedgwood (Light Blue), Coeruleum Blue, Ultramarine and Prussian Blue

Reds

Cadmium Orange, Cadmium Red, Venetian Red, Alizarin Crimson and Indian Red

Whites and Black

Zinc White, Titanium White, Payne's Grey (used to tone colours) and Mars Black
(used rarely)

I have a few ready mixed greens available to use, these are mostly used to mix other colours; I tend to mix greens from the blues and yellows in my pallet.

Golden acrylics colour chart.

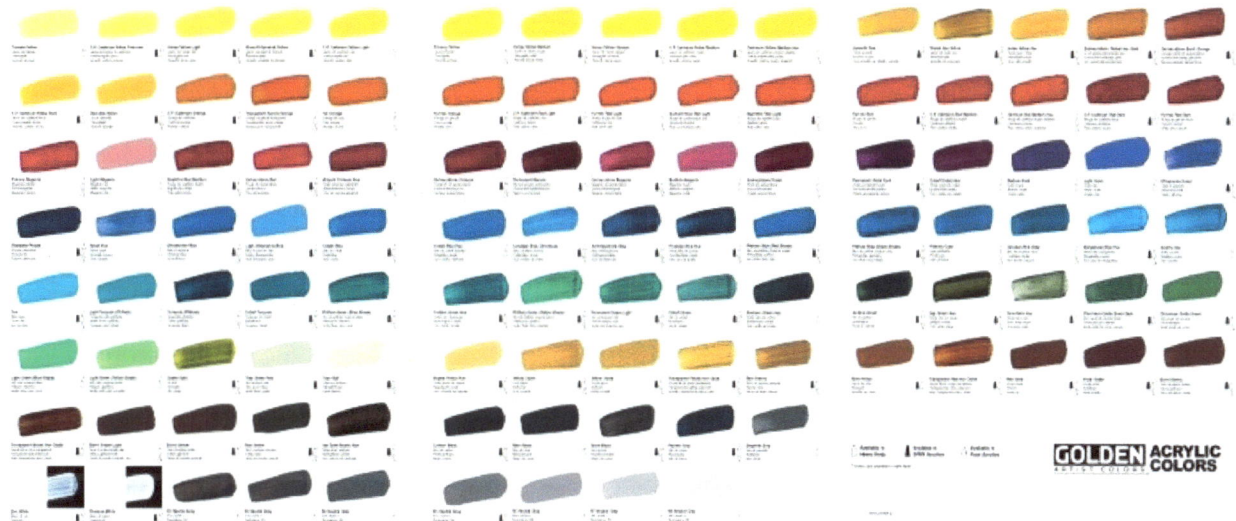

Golden produce 102 colours in their range. Whether you would need to have all of them to hand is a question to ask, but if you did your range of colour mixes would be enormous.

Mixing Surfaces

Your choice of mixing surface is really up to you as there are a great deal of ready made pallets on the market, mostly they are variants of stay wet pallets and white plastic.

Stay Wet pallet

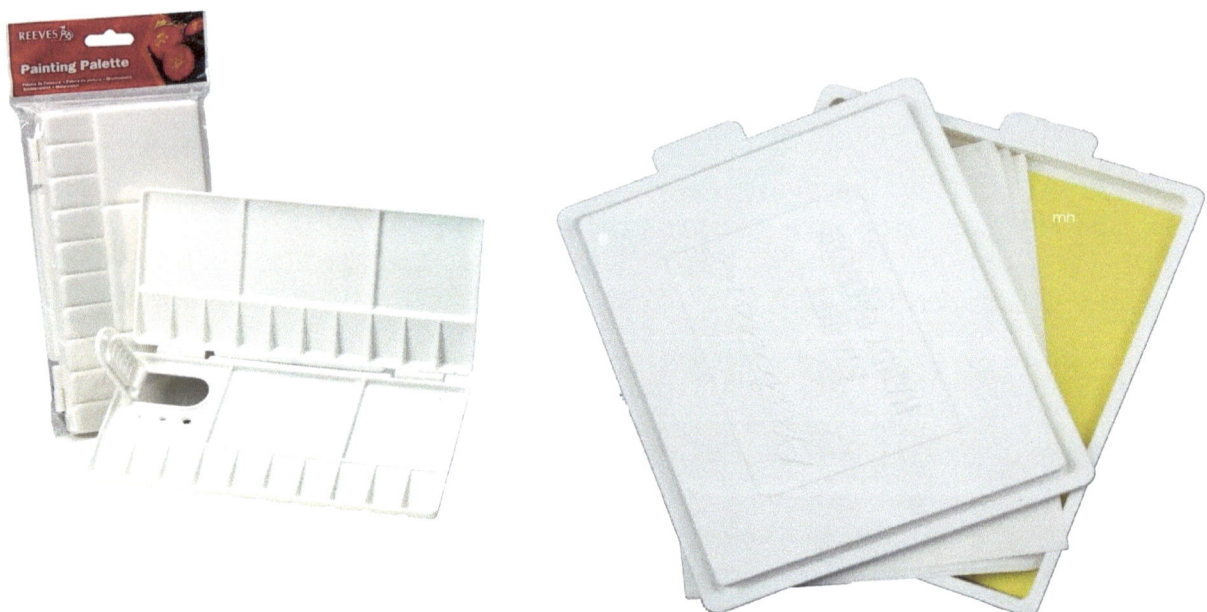

This is a plastic pallet with a sealable lid, the paint sits on a membrane which is on top of a wet sponge, this keeps the paint wet and usable for a period of time. Ideal for eeping mixed colour for later use. Because of the membrane I would not recommend mixing paint with a pallet knife as this could pierce the membrane.

White plastic pallets

These come in many shapes and sizes with space for your paint and a mixing surface.

I use a flat surface to mix on, made from an off-cut of window board. You can use glass, Formica, plastic or MDF and plywood as long as it is sealed to mix your paint on.

I store some of my mixed colour in a stay wet pallet for the duration of a painting in case I need to use that colour again. It is always best to mix more of a colour than you need as you never know if you are going to need more for your picture and mixing the colour again will not completely match.

Washing brushes and cleaning up

Keeping your brushes clean is very important, as the acrylic paint can build up and harden in the brush very quickly.

Keep plenty of water to hand, as you will be constantly washing your brushes, try having two water containers, one for washing the brushes the other for adding water to your colours.

To keep your brushes in perfect condition there are on the market various brush conditioners. If you are painting regularly I recommend using a brush cleaner every now and then to keep your brushes in tip top condition.

My cleaning equipment consists of a collapsible water pot, Brush cleaner and plenty of soft cloths.

I also use a variety of recycled water containers so that I have a plenty full amount of clean water when painting.

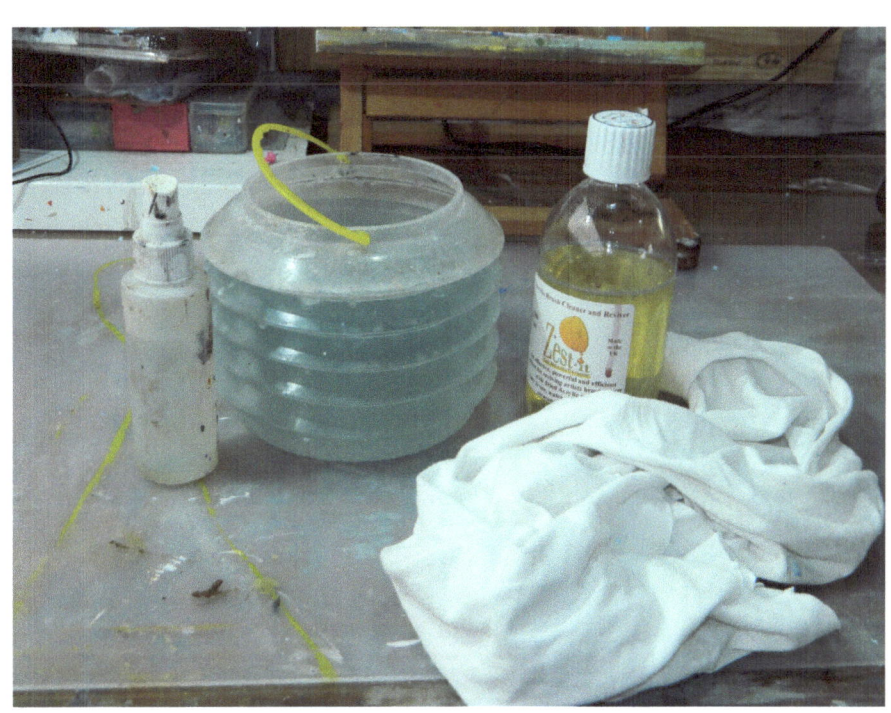

The brush cleaner I use is from Zest it, there are other types available and it is worth asking at your local art store for advice on what is best for your brushes.

I cannot emphasise enough about keeping your brushes in good condition, brushes will over time collect paint at the base of the bristles which makes the brush less flexible and eventually unusable.

So make it a habit to regularly inspect your brushes and give them a deep clean.

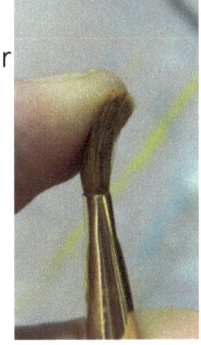 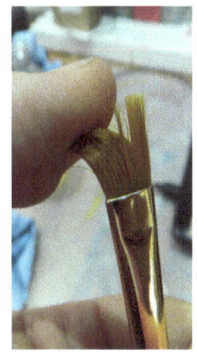

Before and After cleaning

Colour Theory

This is a big subject and I recommend some independent reading on the subject, so I will only touch on the salient points here.

We are taught at an early age that from the 3 primary colours we can produce orange, green and purple and with the addition of white and black we can produce all of the colours we see.

In theory you could restrict your pallet to these colours, but you will struggle to produce vibrant secondary and intermediate colours. Some of the mixes will appear muddy and flat.

How many of us who have tried that and been disappointed by the results, we will look at the colour wheel and try and work out what went wrong.

Well nothing actually went wrong. By restricting your range to just Red, Blue and Yellow with White and Black you are restricting the range of colour mixes you can make.

In reality we need to have a range of Yellows, Reds and Blues. Let's look at the Colour wheel on the next page. .

The colour wheel

Yellow sits between Blue and red so the shades of yellow range from orange yellows to green yellows, Blue range from Blue green to Blue violet and Red between Red Orange and Red Violet.

The Primary colours Red, Blue and Yellow are mixed to make Secondary colours and Intermediate colours are made by the secondary and primary Colours mixed together.

The colours on the wheel are split into two groups, Warm and Cool. Reds and Yellows are seen as warm colours, green and blues are seen as cool colours

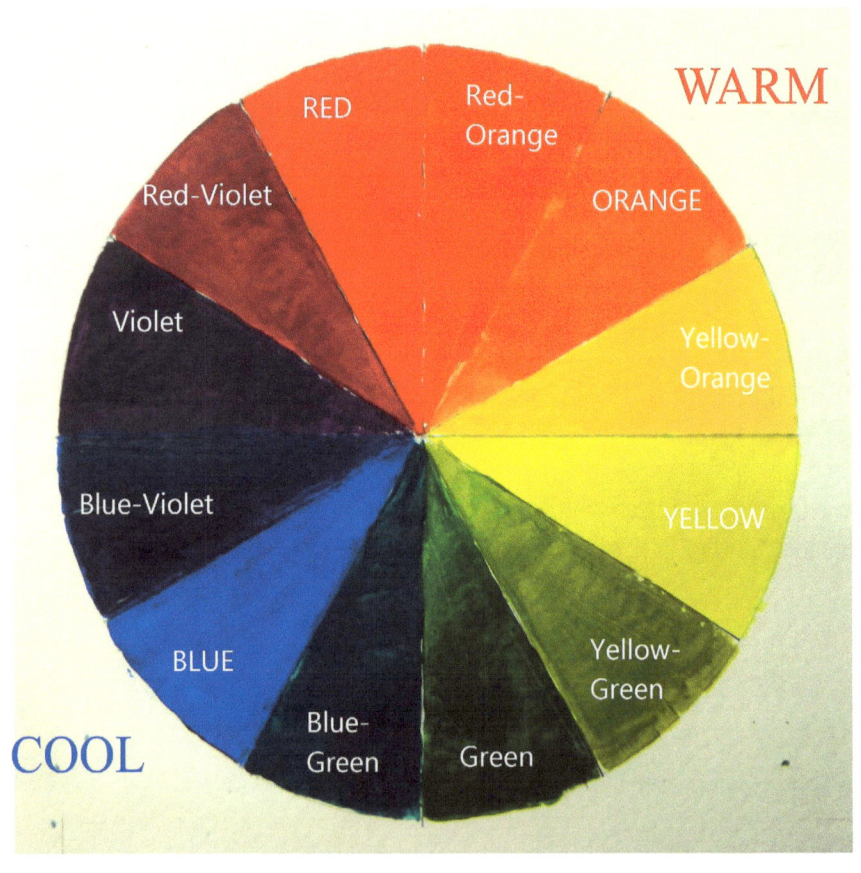

By having a larger range of colours on the pallet we are able to mix far more and more vibrant colours than just by having the 3 primary colours. Also by Tinting or Shading (adding Black) we can lighten or darken any colour we can mix.

Tinting can also be done by simply adding water to the mix as is used in Watercolour painting.

Lets talk more about colour schemes.

Complimentary colours

Where the two colours opposite each other on the colour wheel.

Works best with warm colours against cool colours provides a high contrasting colour scheme.

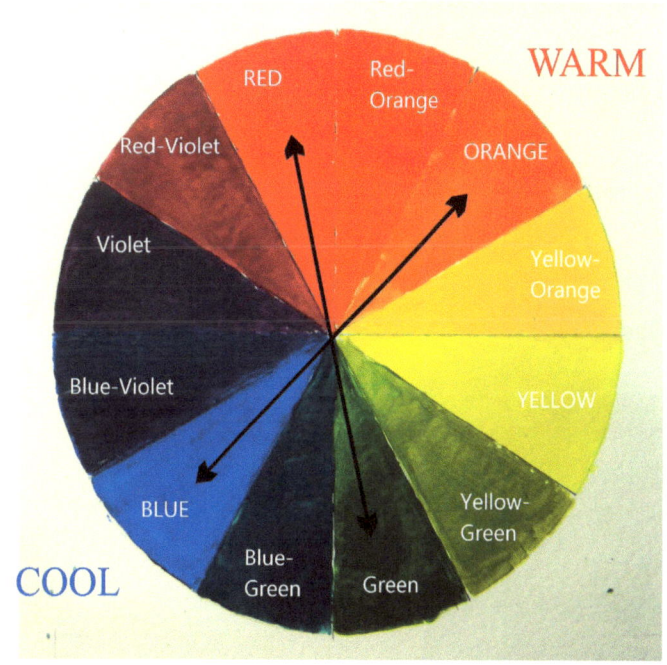

Triadic Colour scheme.

Using 3 colours equally spaced around the colour wheel.

This scheme is popular as offers a strong visual contrast, although not as visual as the 2 colour complimentary but it looks more balanced.

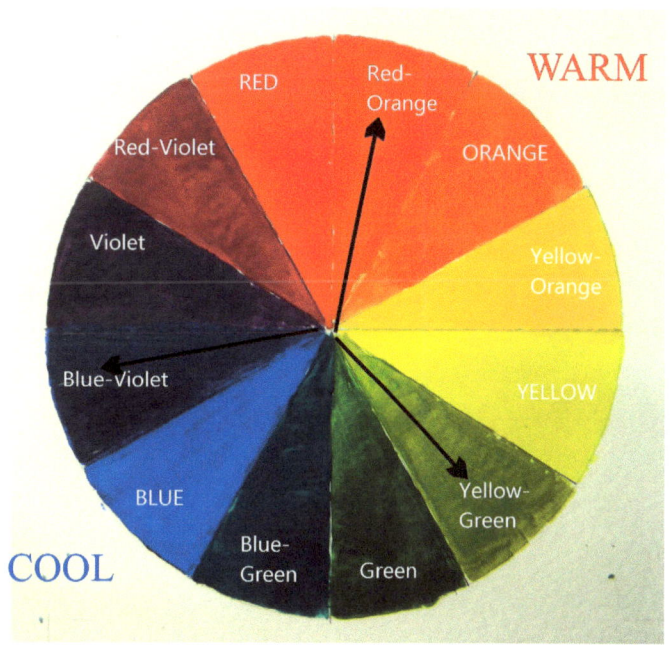

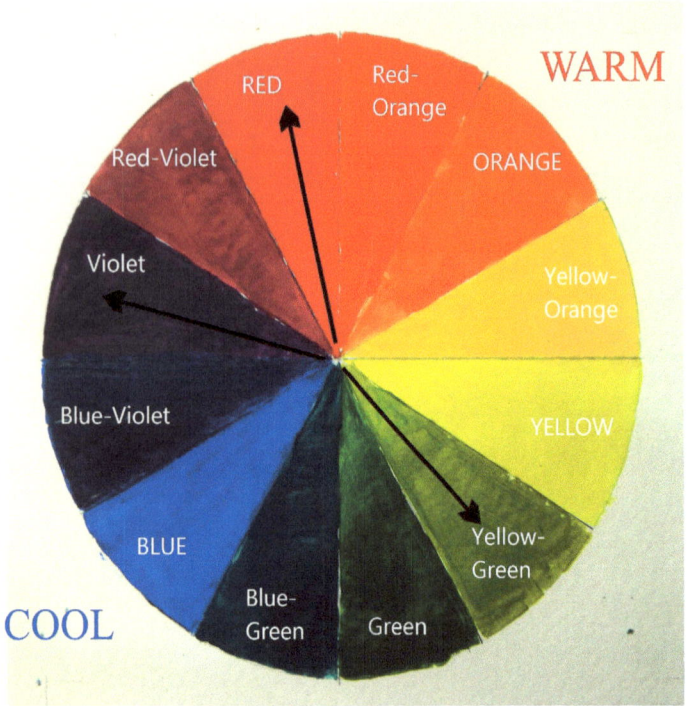

Split complimentary Colour scheme.

A variation of the standard complimentary scheme. It uses one colour and the two adjacent complimentary Colours.

This gives a high contrast with out the strong contrast of the complimentary scheme.

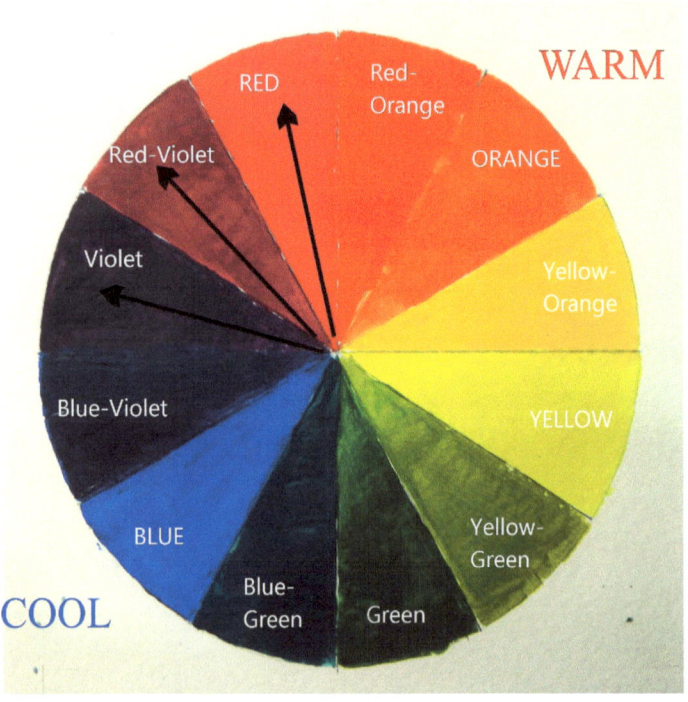

Analogous Colour scheme.

One colour is used as a dominant colour. The others are used to enrich the scheme.

Try looking at other artists work and see if you can see what colour scheme they have used in their paintings.

It is good practice to look at the world around you with your artists eye, and see if you can pick what what sort of colours you can identify. What colours are dominant, and where contrasting colours are used, and take time to look at shadows, see what colours make up shadows.

Keep a camera with you and take photos of things that interest you so that you can go back to the images at a later time.

That's enough of colour theory for now. Lets start messing with paint.

Mixing colour
Do's and Dont's
When mixing colour on your pallet use a Pallet Knife rather than your brush, the brush will get overloaded with paint and the paint will be forced down to the stem of the bristles and be hard to clean, residual paint will harden and render the brush useless. If you do mix with a brush thoroughly clean it straight away.

Mixing on the canvas can be done with a knife, scraper, brush or any other implement you may wish to use, I find that fingers are very good for this.

Optical mixing can be done with washes of colour overlaying a base colour with the light bouncing of the base colour mixing with the wash, some very subtle effects can be made this way.

Knowing what colours you can mix from your pallet of colours is fairly important, no one can remember how they mix certain hues, I always have a mixing chart showing what I can make from the mix.

It is time for you to have a go and start experimenting.

Mixing colours and colour charts

In this exercise I want you to start experimenting with mixing colours. I have completed the colour chart shown below. The paint that I have used is Daler-Rowney System 3: Lemon Yellow, Cadmium Yellow, Cadmium Red, Crimson, Ultramarine, Emerald Green, Yellow Ochre, Burnt Umber, Mars Black. These are the colours I have mixed from a standard 10 colour starter set.

By mixing one colour with another and also making a tint of the resulting colour by adding white.

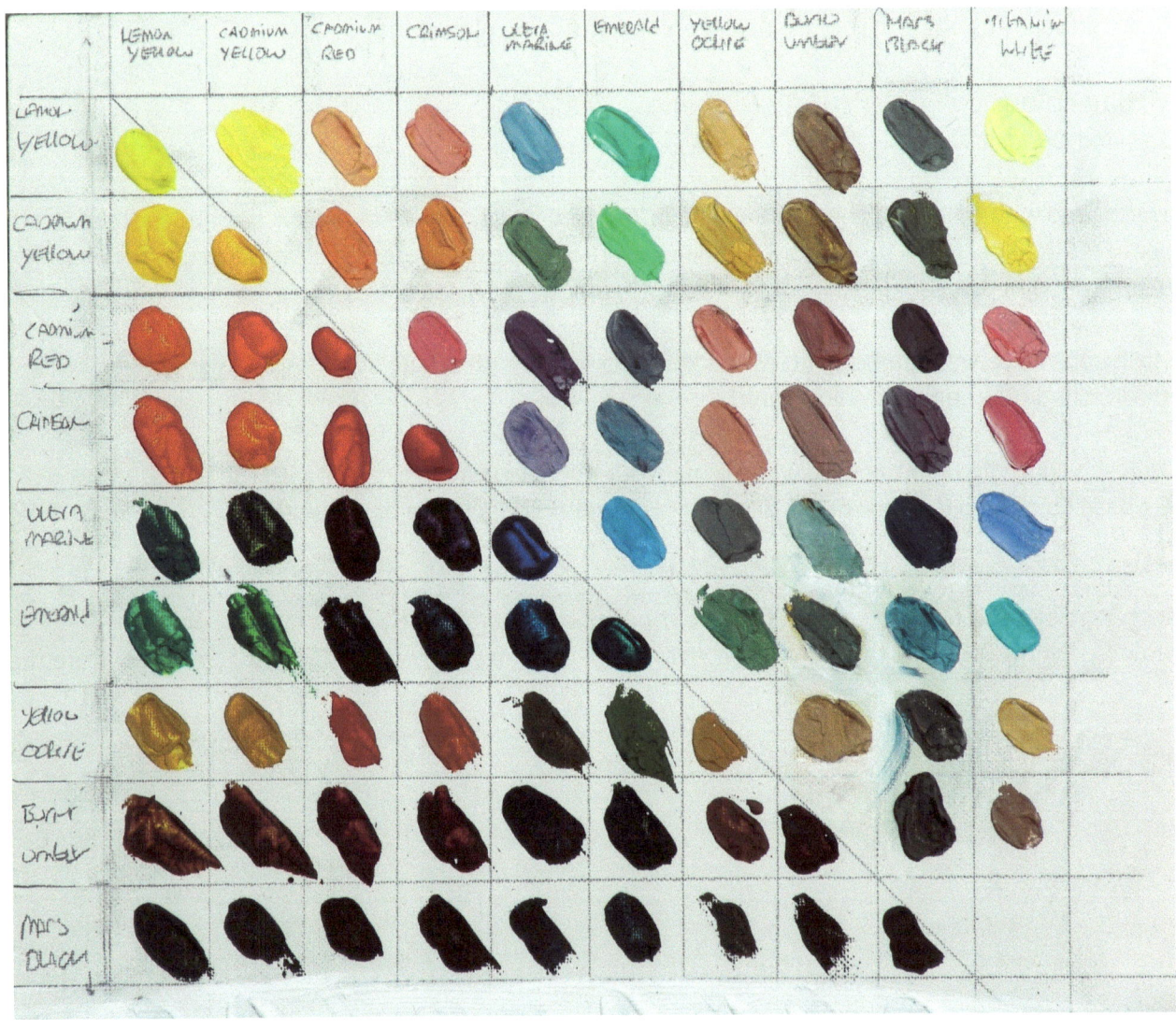

It is interesting to see what you can mix, by adding 2 colours together we have made a further 36 secondary colours by adding a small amount of white makes a total of 82 colours available.

But there is pretty much 1000's of tints and shades you can mix from these colours.

Now it is your turn.
Exercise 1 Making a colour chart
Have a go at making your own colour chart using the paint colours available to you. You can add more colours if you wish, try and have 3 shades of each primary as in the colour wheel we looked at earlier, see how many mixes you can get.

Another good exercise is to mix a colour and progressively add water or white to the mix to tint the colour.
A chart showing tints of colours by progressively adding white.

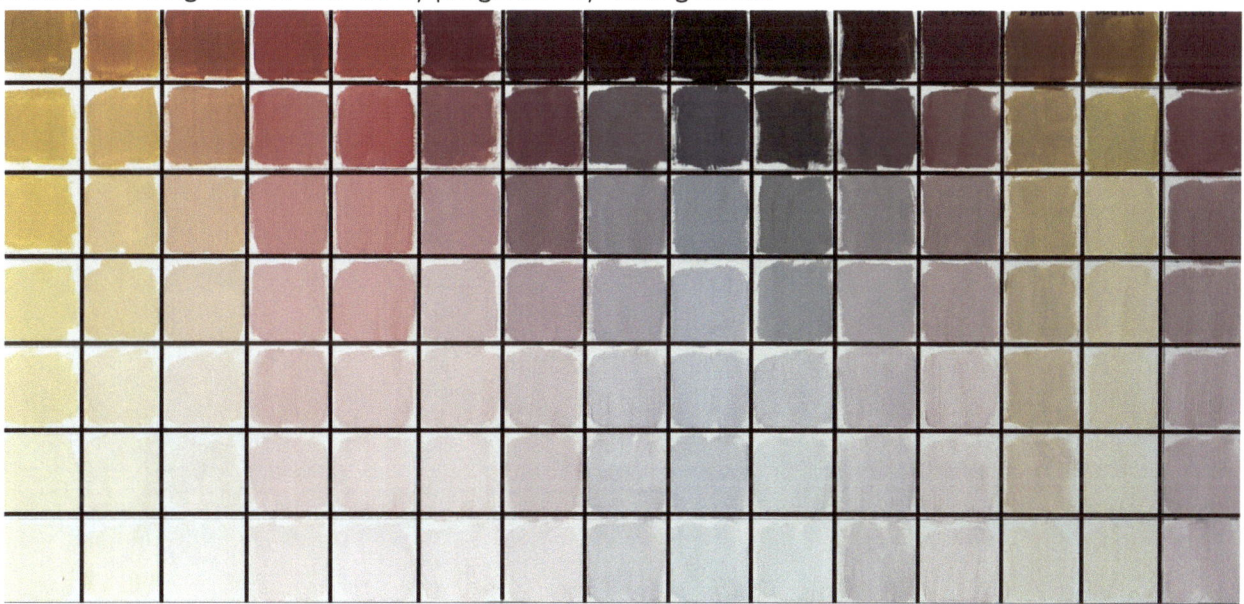

Making your own colour chart is a very good exercise to do, no one can remember all the colours that you can make or how to make them, this is also a good way of showing you what range of colours that you can make and will highlight any gaps you may want to fill.

When buying paints, be aware that paints from different manufacturers may share the same name but may not have the same composition of pigments. Try to use paints from one manufacturer only. And when you add more colours to your range do some more experimenting with mixes.

Now you have some idea about colour and mixing different colours from your pallet, lets look at the basic techniques you will find useful when painting with acrylics .

Technique 1: Optically mixing colour

A technique used in Oil painting that lends its self to Acrylics because of the quick drying time between application of the layers of paint in glazes.

How it works

Optical mixing is a way of building up a rich colour on your painting by the application of colour mixed with acrylic glaze or in a wash with water to make the colour more transparent and allows the base colour to shine through. The light bouncing off the lower layer mixes with the colour of the wash or glaze changing the colour that you see.

By using multiple layers you will get an effect so unlike using opaque paints, the depth and richness to the colours you achieve with each layer adding to the effect and changing the colours below.

You can use this technique over thicker layers of paint as well as flat colour. This technique really lets you play with optically mixing colour on the canvas, and is best used with a glazing medium as the colours will be more vibrant and transparent.

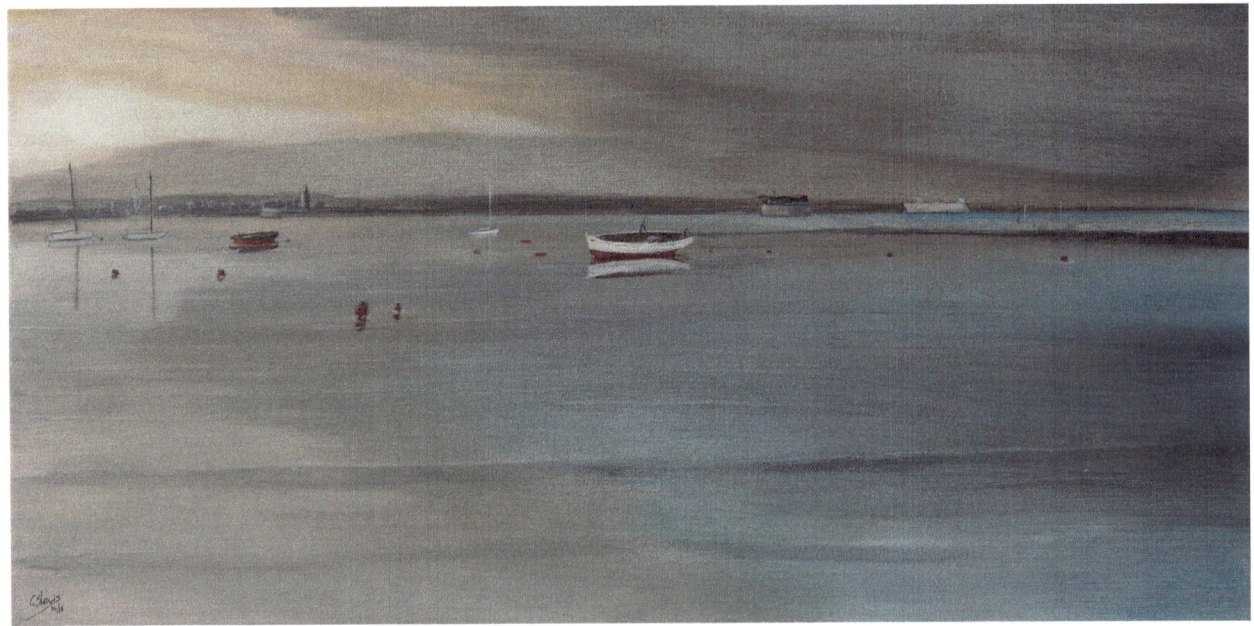

Solent from Seaview by Geoff Lewis

This is a good example of the use of optical mixing. I started with a wash of Yellow Ochre and built up the layers of colour using washes with the detail added last, the picture has a luminosity that I could not have done any other way.

Exercise 2 Optical mixing

Have a look at your colour chart.

We can make another colour chart but this time optically mixing the colours.

Not every mix is going to achieve a good result but persevere as this chart will be very useful too you going forward.

So lets get started, on your original chart we have one half for the full mix and the other adding white.

This time mix one half with the lighter colours over dark then the other half darker colours over light as the colours mix differently either way. Do this with a wash of each colour not paint straight from the tube.

Glazing is another technique for optically mixing colour, this is done using an acrylic glaze in a mix on your pallet this makes the colour more transparent, it also increases the drying time making the paint more workable. I will discuss this technique later in the book.

The changes in colours are subtle in this example, but you can see what changes can occur when mixing colour this way on your picture.

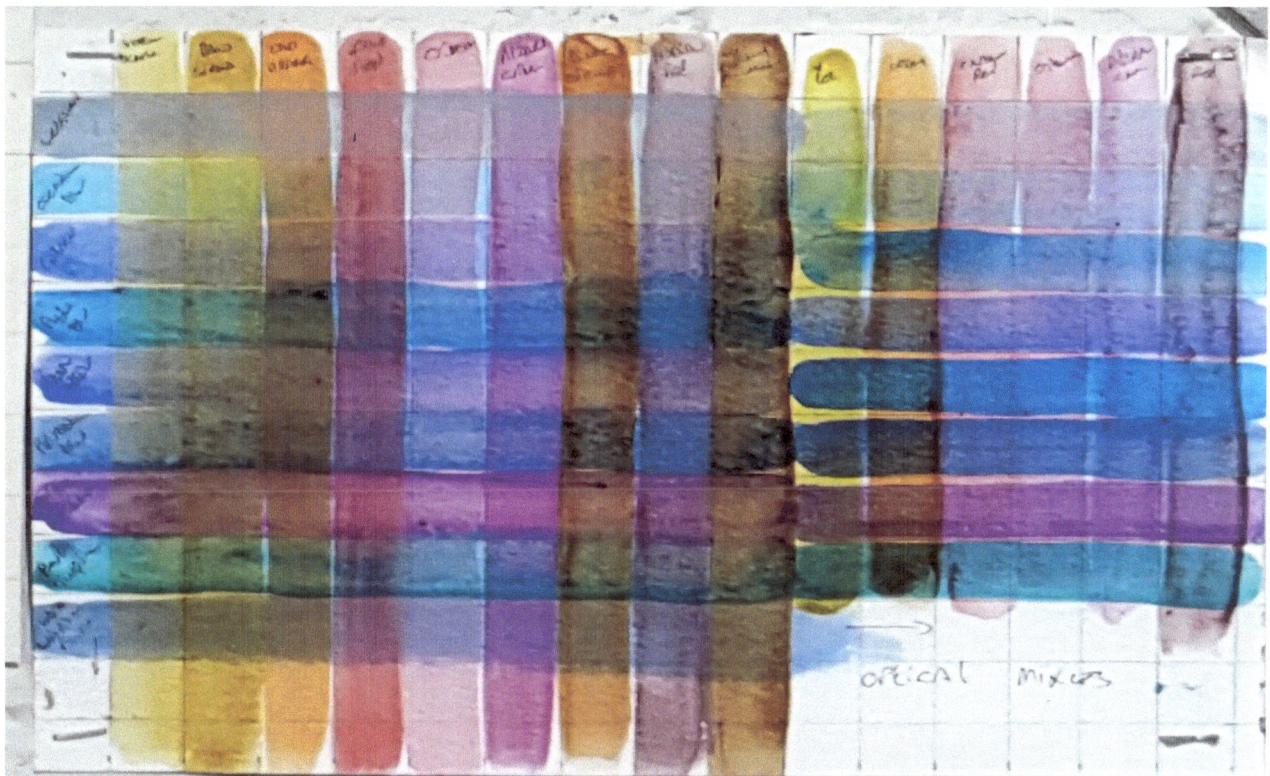

Optical colour chart

Technique 2: Blending

Blending is the technique of merging one colour with another, so that the colours appear to seamlessly blend together.

Blending colour is the main reason that people don't like acrylics because of the quick drying time there is not a great deal of time to do this on the canvas. However blending can be achieved fairly easily. Lets look at the techniques we can use.

If you are using your paints as washes, as in watercolours. You can blend colours by keeping the canvas wet in the area you want to blend, adding the second colour over this area the colours diffuse into each other. This is known as a wet on wet technique and can also be achieved with a slow drying or retarding medium in the paint mix or painted onto the canvas before painting. This gives a longer working time so you can blend your colours to the precision you want. (See Wet on Wet)

Using a water spray can also keep the paint wet on your canvas and is also useful in keeping your paints workable on your pallet especially if it is hot where you are working.

Here is an example for you to work with.

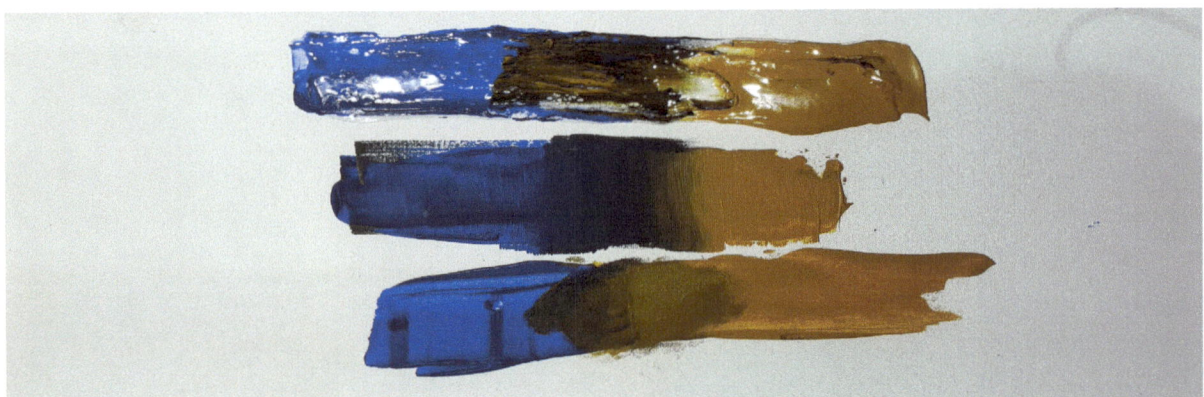

The top bar is using a slow drying medium directly applied to the canvas with the paint being applied by painting knife and roughly blended in using the knife (see Wet in Wet).

The second bar is paint direct from the tube being blended with a dry brush using quick vertical brush strokes giving a soft blend of the two colours.

Lastly I have let the two colours nearly dry and scumbled a colour over the join with a wet finger.

Exercise 3 Blending Colour

On your practice paper repeat the process I have used using colours of your choice, if the paint is drying to quickly use a mister to spray some water onto the paint this will increase the working time. You may want to come back to this exercise a few times to get the hang of the technique.

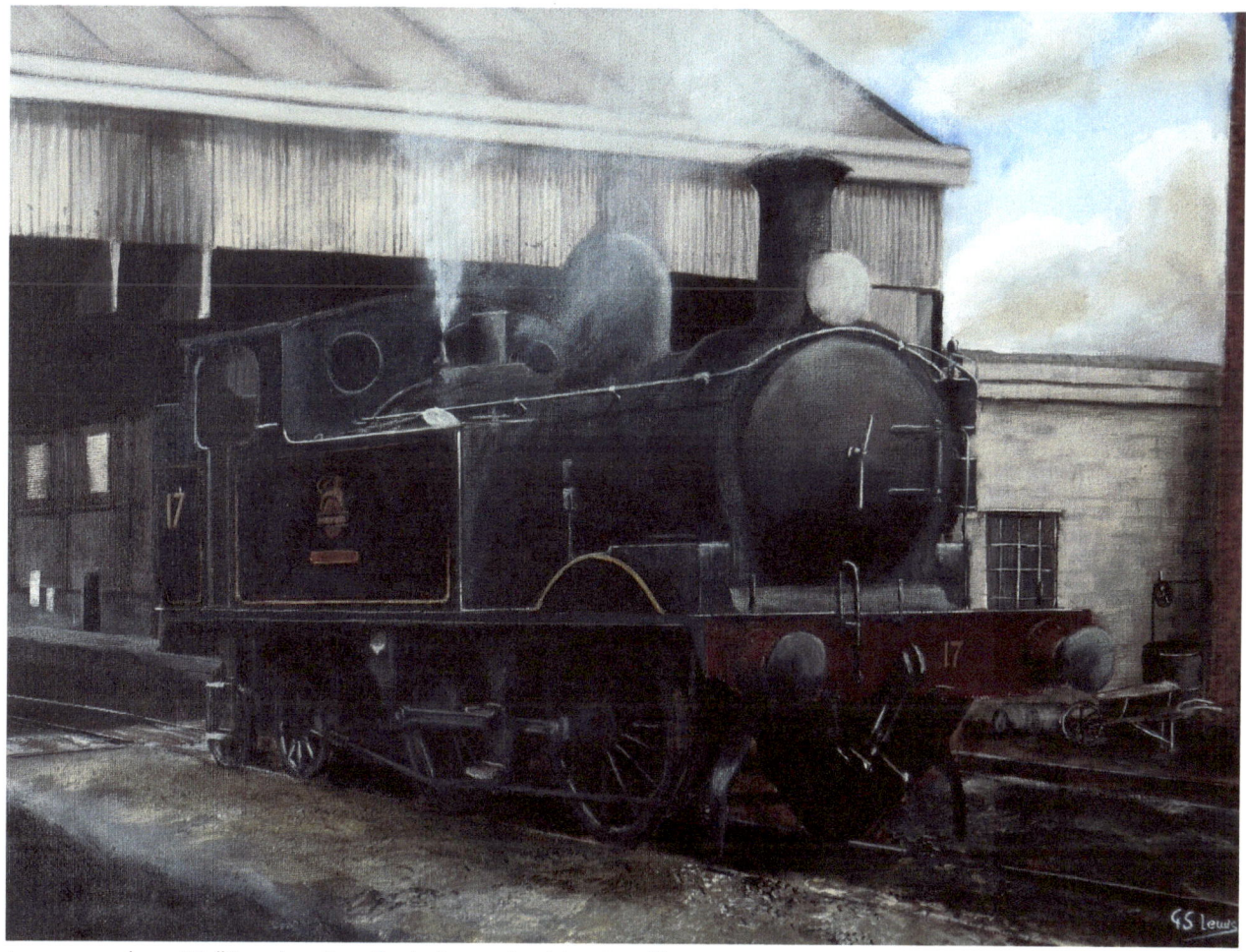

Loco number 17 "Seaview" at Ryde loco shed by Geoff Lewis

No matter what you are painting there will always be a need to blend areas of colour. It would not be possible to make this image without being able to blend the colours together, this picture is a good example of using colour to show shape and form. Adding highlights using the lighter shades and contrasting with the pools of darker paint gives form and brings the picture to life.

Using light and shadow to show form is an essential tool for the artist, I particularly enjoy getting to the point in a painting where I am able to paint in the highlights, this really brings everything to life.

Technique 3: Using Coloured Grounds

Most painters like to paint a coloured ground on the canvas, this eliminates white spaces and can effect the mood of the painting. It is also useful for beginners as it can be difficult to asses colours against the white background.

Using coloured grounds also helps with not leaving patches of unpainted surface, the colour of the ground shows through and can unify the painting.

So what colours should you use?

I, as a default use yellow ochre, as it is works well for the light of most of the day, but what colour you choose for your painting is up to you and the subject matter.

You may want to have a contrasting or complimentary ground, it really does depend on the subject. As a guide for landscapes and seascapes tone your canvas for the time of day, Yellow Ochre works well for daylight, but for warm summer mornings use a brighter yellow but not Lemon Yellow as this is too bright and hard to establish depth in the painting.

Summer evenings use a more orange tint and sunsets try some reds, as with this painting of Ryde sands.

For colder days and late evenings have a go with warm greys this compliments the colder colours in the painting.

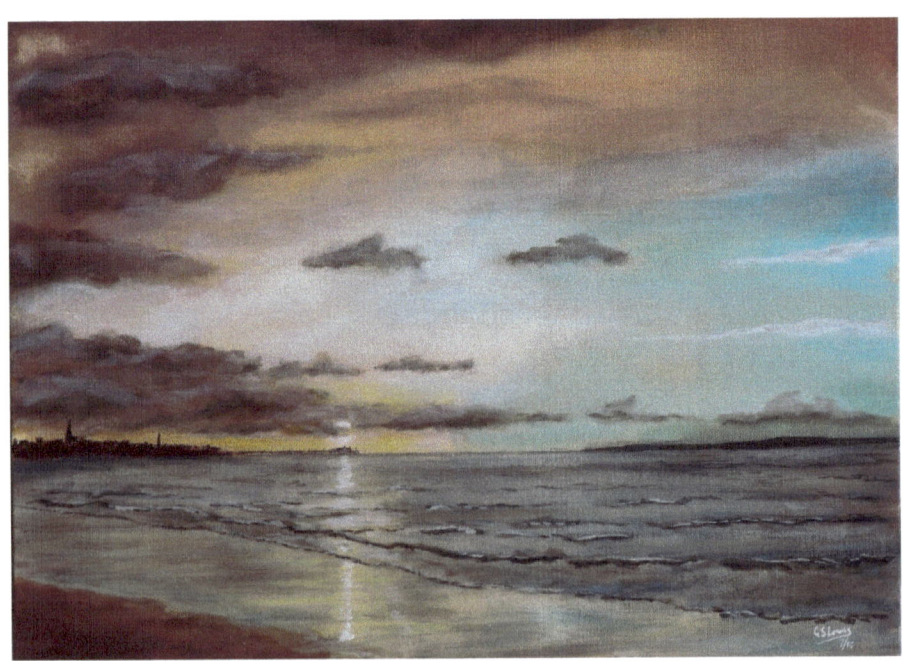

Ryde Sands by Geoff Lewis

Also have a good look at your subject matter, see what colour dominates your subject then look at the complimentary or the contrasting colours on the colour wheel to help you. Do bear in mind that it is not just the colour of the ground that will effect your painting, try using a mid colour tone (or tint) as you can then work with darker and lighter tones of the colour in your painting.

Technique 4: Glazing - Using Acrylic glazing medium

Glazing is a layer of transparent paint, either thick or used as a wash which lets the underlying paint surface to show through. This is another way of optically mixing colour. To produce a glaze you need a glazing medium, this can be purchased from your local art shop.

Glazing medium is different from Acrylic medium. Glazing medium is a milky liquid that dries clear and to a gloss finish, whereas Acrylic medium is more thicker and dries to an opaque white. You can use the Glazing medium without any colour to make a clear glaze, letting light bounce between the coloured glazes, this method can produce some beautiful luminous skies. Glazing is an integral part of painting, it has been used for hundreds by year by the great masters. JMW Turner used glazes in his skies to achieve luminosity that cannot be gained by just using paint alone.

You don't have to limit your glazes on just flat paint, you can glaze over impasto surfaces as well.

Exercise 4: Painting of a Glazed Jug.

Using the picture here we are going to produce a painting using glazes.

I am going to walk you through this exercise stage by stage.

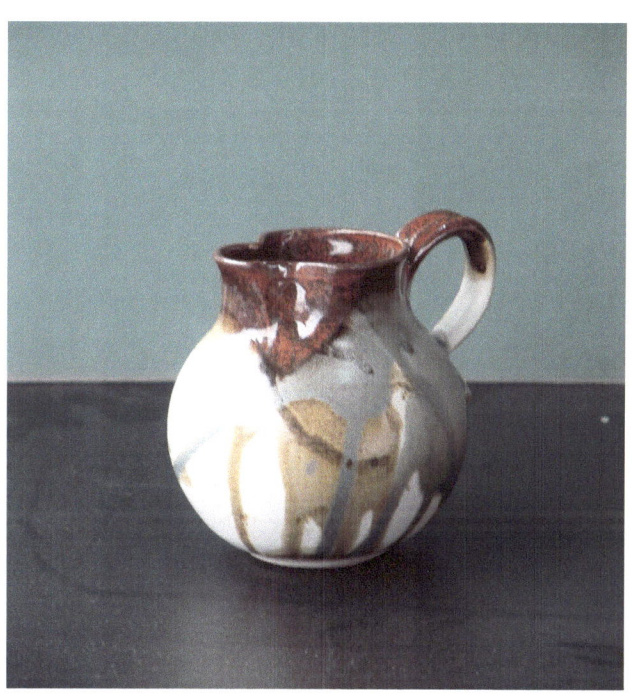

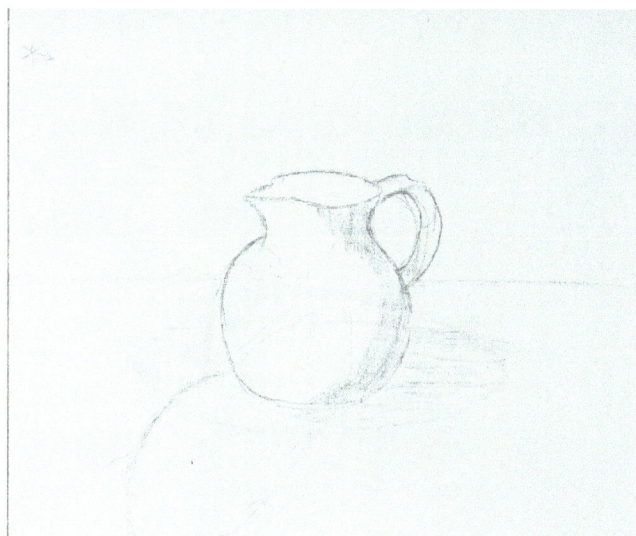

Start with a drawing, there is no need for complete accuracy, use light pencil marks to describe the shape.

Then decide on your background colours use a light wash rather than full colour, then paint the jug with a base colour of Yellow Ochre tinted with White.

Let everything dry we don't want the base colour mixing with the glaze we are going to add.

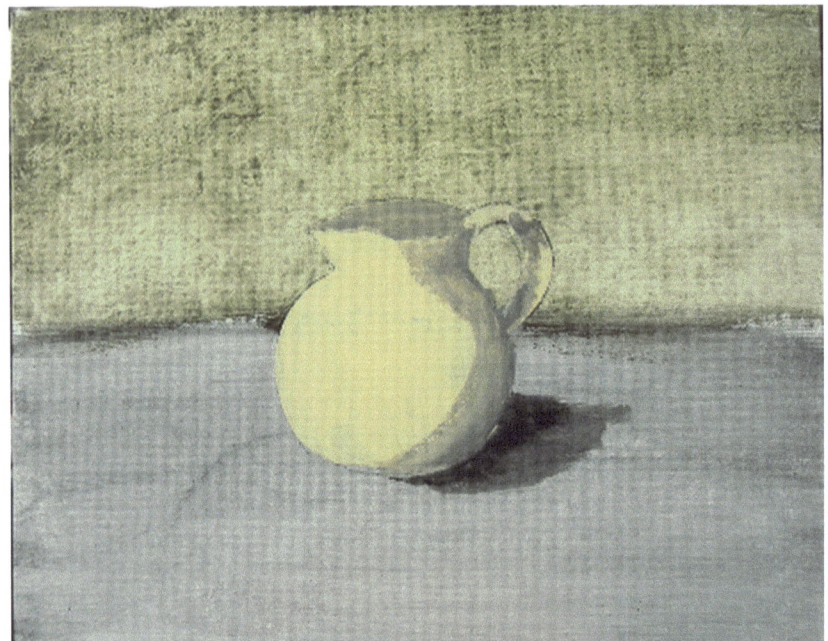

I used a mix of Ultramarine and Yellow Ochre with some water to give an olive green shade, applied with the ¾ flat brush, then blotted out with hand towel to give some texture. By adding some black to this mix we get a grey shade add some water to make a wash and this time wipe the wash off with the paper towel.

Now for the glazed layers

Using Yellow Ochre and White to make a light tint mixed with an equal amount of Glazing Medium, I painted the under glaze, then mixing a grey (Ultramarine and Orange), I added the next glaze. Don't forget to let your layers dry completely or you will get a muddy mess. If you do, don't worry because once dry you can start again with the base colour, that's the advantage of acrylic paint.

For the darker glaze I started with Burnt Sienna Mixed with a very small spot of Black, and then over 3 more glazes I lightened the colour with the last being a White glaze for the reflections.

If you want, try using different colours, you don't have to stick to the colours of your subject.

Glazing is a technique you can use in many situations.

I always use glazing in skies and water, you can put a layer of glaze between layers of paint, I find this useful if I am optically mixing colour using washes. The glazed layer lets the light bounce between the colour washes increasing the depth and luminosity of the colours.

When you look at your chosen subject, do consider whether you could use glazing in parts of your painting, still life painting is a good example where glazing works well, polished fruit, glass and reflections all lend themselves to this technique.

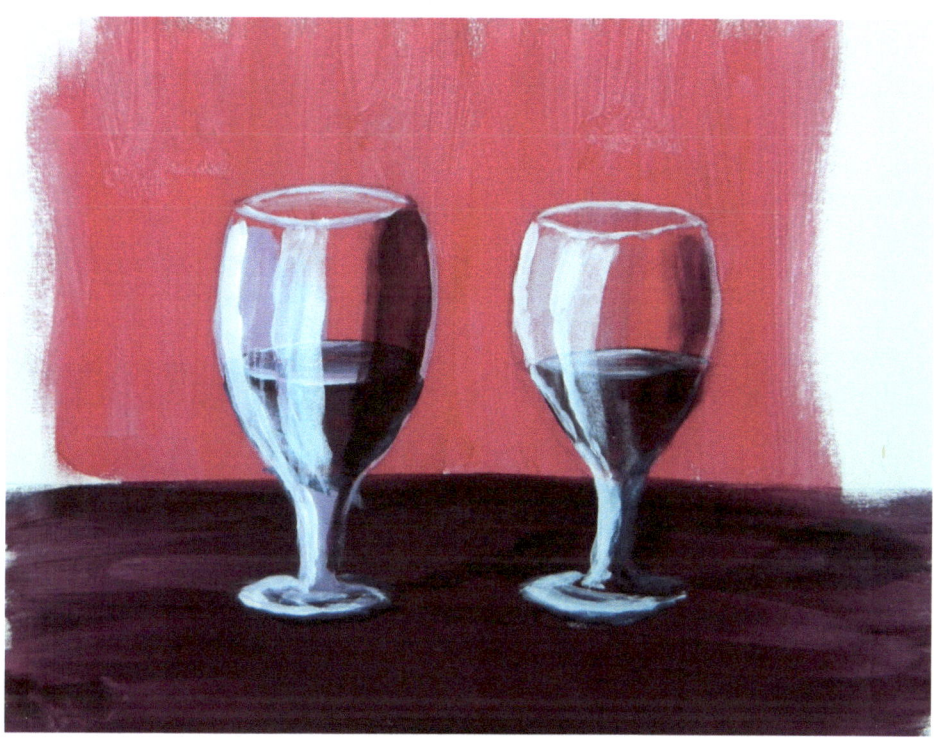

This is a very quick sketch of a pair of wine glasses just to show the difference between using solid paint and using glazes.

The glass on the left was painted with solid paint and looks more solid compared to the glass on the right which looks more opaque. Try this yourself.

Practice painting reflections using glazes then repeat the picture without using this technique. You will be surprised by the difference.

Technique 5: Pallet knives and painting knives

There is a distinction between pallet knives and painting knives. A pallet knife has a long flat blade whereas a painting knife has a bend in the shank of the knife to keep your hand above the painting surface. I personally use both types when painting.

Painting with knives is an expressive way of applying paint to a surface, paint with
a brush can be applied thick or thin, with a knife it will always be applied thick.

Painting can be done quickly and expressively, slow and deliberate or combination of both, colours can be mixed on the painting surface or on the pallet. With a painting
knife you can lay down a layer of paint that is smooth that once dry will reflect the light and give a perfect rendition of colour, or as textured as you like to give movement and structure with an impasto technique.

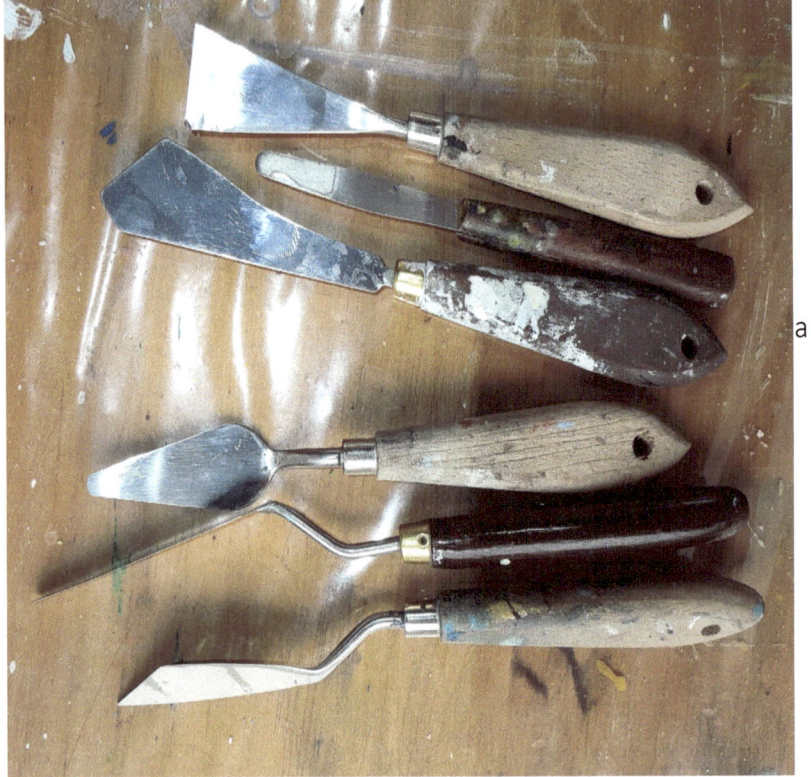

a

Using thick paint also means that the paint will take longer to dry and you will have more time to work blending or scraping out colour to show the surface colours.

Working like this is very liberating, you can quickly produce the effect you want, which you can over paint with a coloured wash or dry brushing or other mediums such soft pastel onto the ridges of the paint or using inks to fill pools of colour in between the ridges once the paint is dry.

The painting on the next page was produced using a painting knife and number 6 round brush plus the odd finger.

Loosely mixing colour on the pallet and letting the colours mix on the painting gives the streaks of colour depicting the dirt and grime on the loco boiler and body. Shape is added by controlling the direction of the knife.

The background contrasts with the dark browns of the loco, making it stand out of the picture. The red figure draws the eye to the focal point in the picture, of the cutter doing his work.

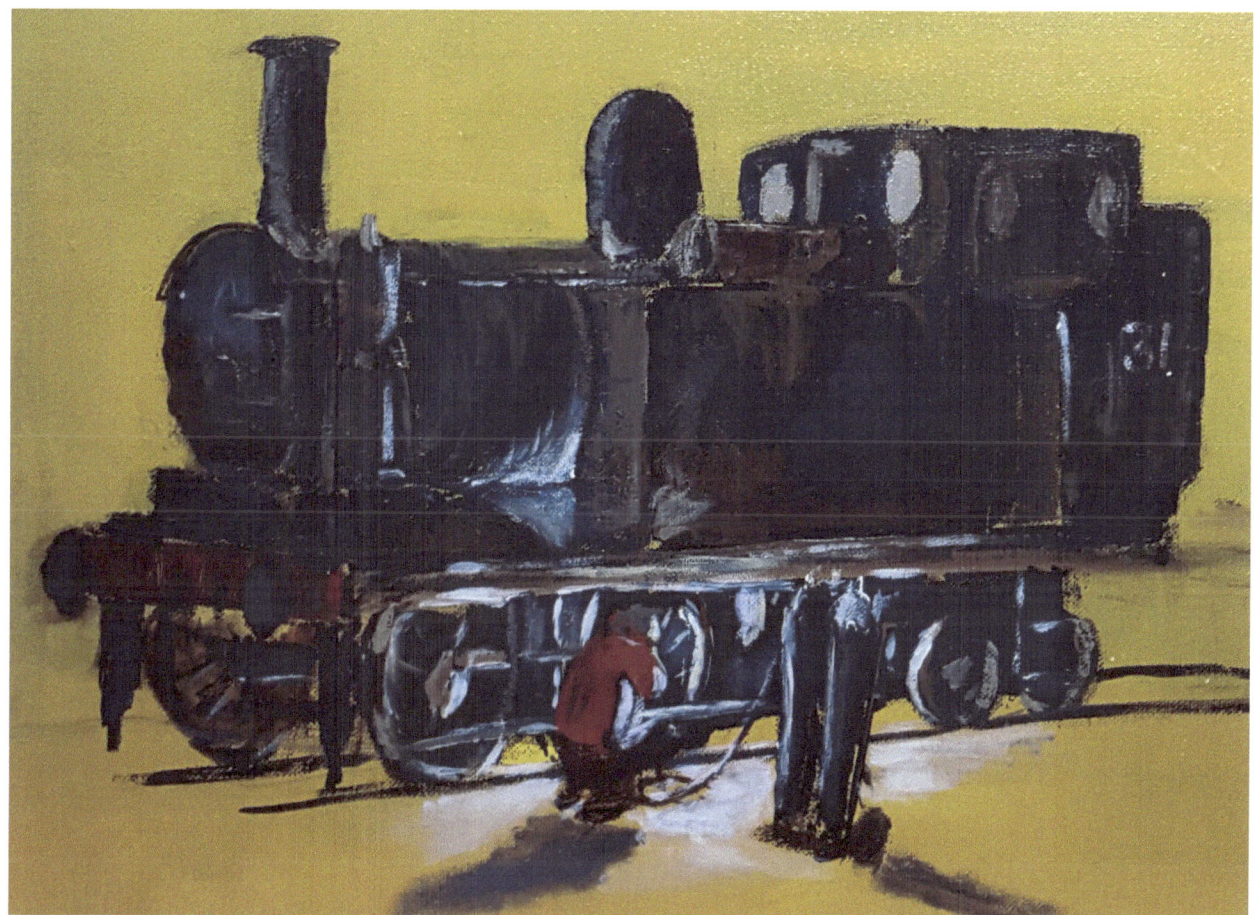

The cutters Torch by Geoff Lewis

Now its your turn again.

Exercise 5 Painting with a Knife or scraper
Using a knife to show shape and form.

Take a piece of practice paper for this exercise.

Lets start with a cylindrical object say a wine bottle or drinks can, use it to draw a quick sketch of a cylinder as a guide, nothing complex we are only playing here. Without adding any background detail just look at the bottle and see what shapes you can see.

Using your painting knife select some colour from your pallet and use the knife to apply colour and describe the shape of the cylinder add colour to the knife to contrast the first colour and use that for the highlights by using vertical strokes.
The blue layer which describes the shape has dried quickly so when I add the vertical highlights the paint catches the ridges in the paint, further emphasizing the shape of the object. I added a strip of

white to give a brighter highlight. The rule here is to be bold, use large quick strokes of the knife be positive, but most of all keep your hand supple.

Using a pallet knife can be very liberating, opening up a loose urgent style of painting you may not have tried before.

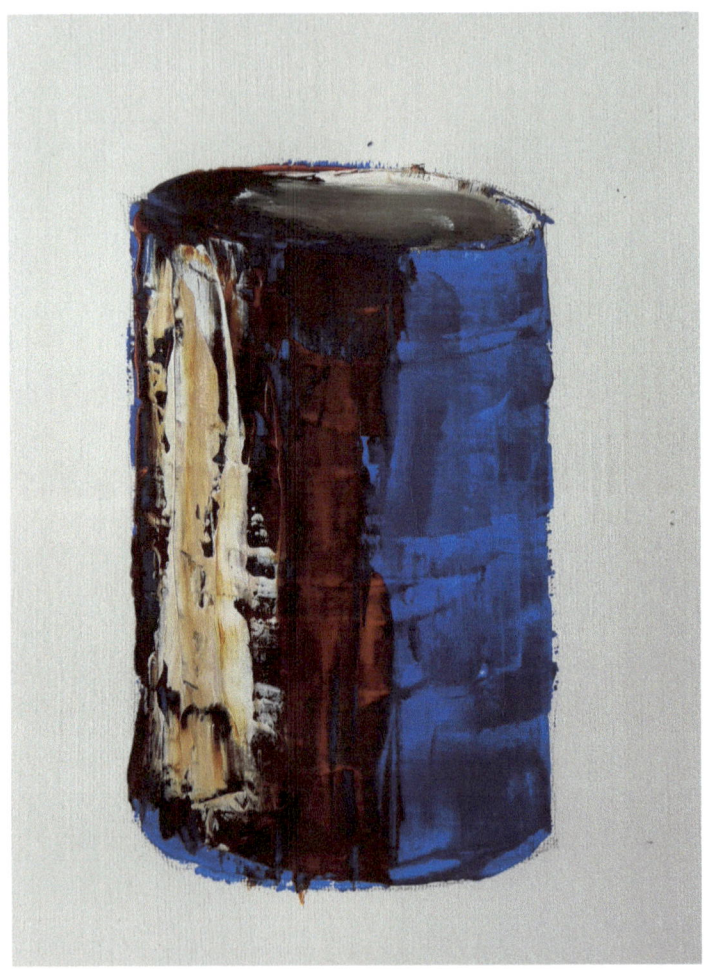

Try painting other shapes, and use different shaped knives as they all produce different effects. Or try making your own knives and scrapers from scrap card or plastic, old credit cards lend themselves to making good scrapers.

I have found kitchen utensils useful when working on a large scale, try looking around your local home store or DIY shop.

Technique 6: Impasto

The word Impasto means paint that has been applied thickly enough to retain the brush marks. Acrylic paint has the right consistency to be painted very thickly, an advantage of acrylic paint is that it does not crack no matter how thick the paint is.

So you can layer up a painting as much as you like, so that it has almost a 3 dimensional look to your picture.

Heavy body paint has a thicker consistency than the standard acrylic paints and is perfect for impasto painting, although you can use a structure gel which thickens the paint giving you the same effect as heavy body paint.

You don't need to restrict yourself to just using brushes, you can use painting knives or scrapers, or even some household items such as combs or whatever else you may want to use to produce the desired effect.

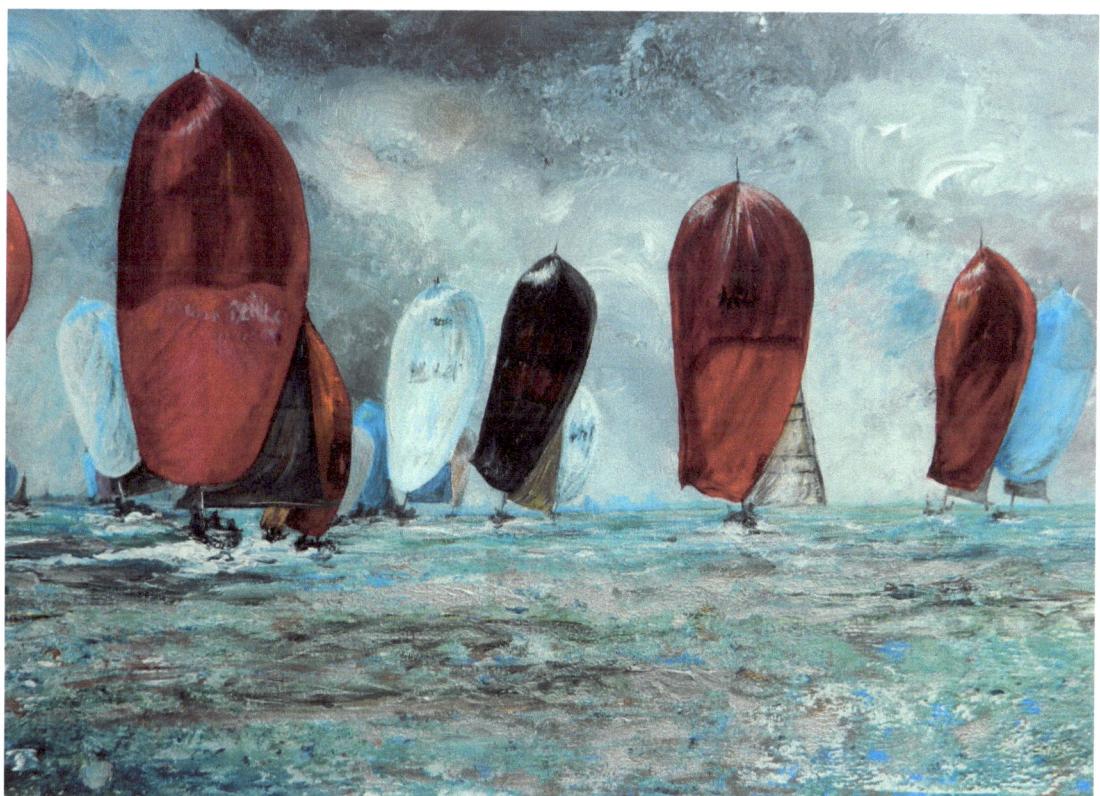

This is part of a painting by Linda Caldicott, which has been painted wet in wet and with a heavy bodied paint. Linda has used Rollers, Combs and brushes to make this picture.

The direction of the brushwork describes the shapes being painted and the peaks of the impasto paint catches the light, making a very atmospheric painting.

Exercise 6. Lets make some marks.

Take a piece of canvas board and paint on a wash of a light grey, use a mix of light blue and orange with a bit of white, yes this does make grey.

Once dried we can start making marks, don't think about painting a picture at this point. We are just experimenting with the technique making marks on the board.

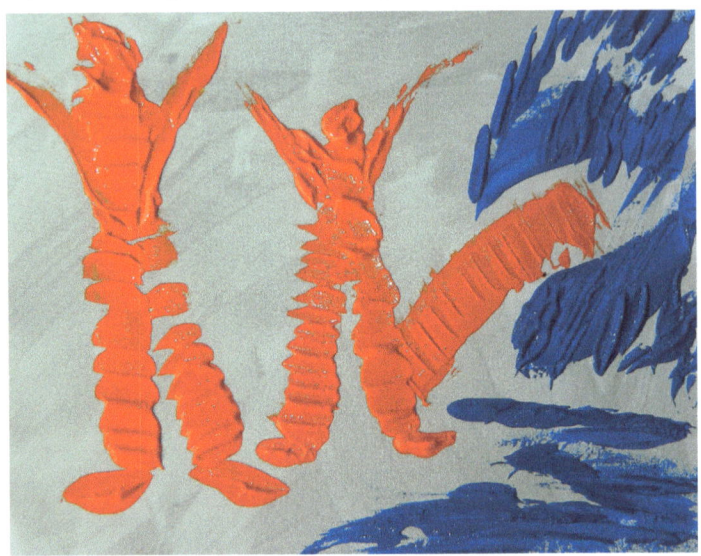

Working like this can be very liberating, be loose and work quickly, let the brush or knife dictate what happens. This is the joy of painting, just playing with techniques and your tools can sometimes produce an effect that you really like.

I have chosen to start with orange as I have it to hand and using a painting knife I have spread a thick textured layer in several places.

Again just playing I have made the shapes into people like forms. Adding some ultramarine to contrast the orange I have again spread a layer of paint with the knife.

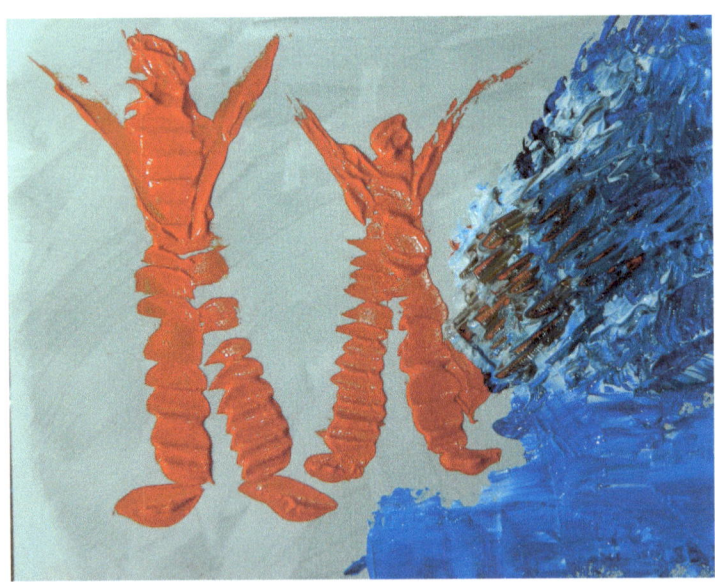

Whilst the paint is still wet lets use the light blue I have to hand make some waves, a bit extra white to lighten up the area and scrape some paint away to show the orange underneath to show movement as you may see in water.

Impasto helps the viewer of your art by describing movement and shape and is a very useful tool in our skills toolbox.

Technique 7: Wet on Wet

This painting is a very good example of impasto as well as wet on wet painting, using rollers and combs to blend colour on the canvas.

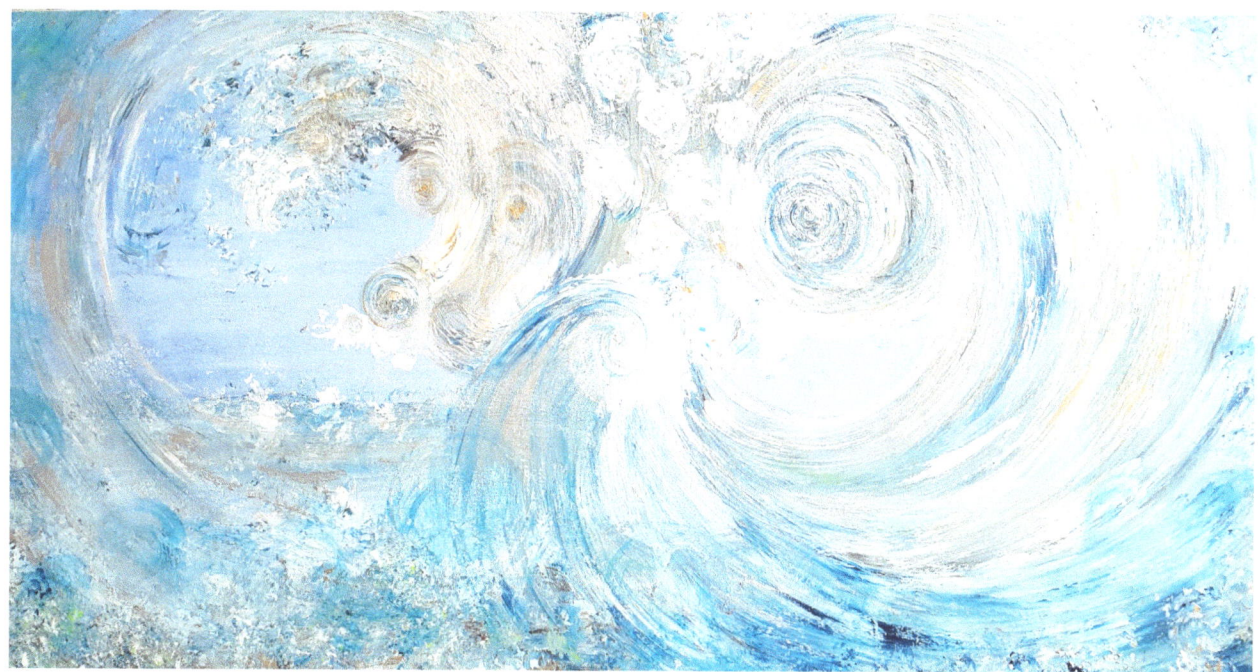

Silver Surf Serpent by Linda Caldicott

This technique involves applying colours over one another blending the colours together on the canvas. Every new application of colour will blend with the others on the canvas giving softer shapes and forms that merge together without any hard edges.

A word of caution try not to over work the paint as it will make the colours muddy and can effect the brushwork that you want to show.

With acrylic paints you can add a retarder to the paint or directly onto the canvas, this will slow the drying time and allow you to work the paint. If things go wrong you can scrape the paint of the surface and start again.

We started using wet on wet with the previous exercise just using paint from the tube, working quickly produced some interesting effects and shapes. Using a softer approach with brushes, you can with the wet in wet technique produce some beautiful effects.

This painting is an example of the effects you can achieve with wet in wet and blending the colours with soft brush strokes.

Using a mop brush to soften the brush strokes, and using quick vertical strokes with a flat brush for the sea, I have produced a very soft effect blending the colours together.

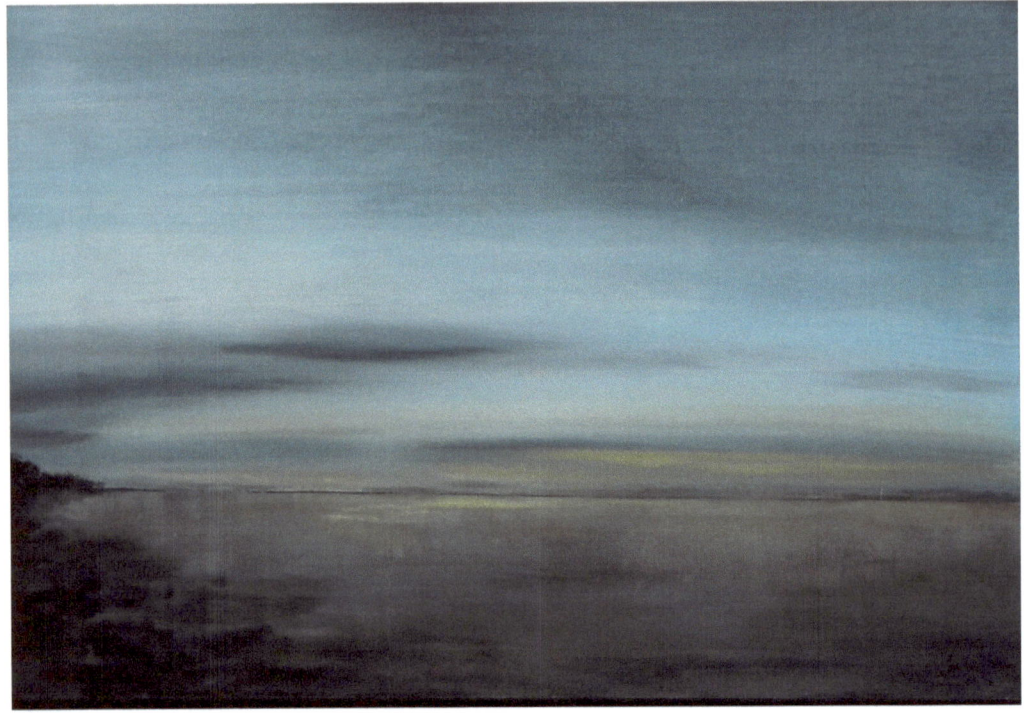

Dusk by Geoff Lewis

Exercise 7: Sea and Sky

We discussed blending earlier in this book so as another exercise I would like you to have a go at a sea and sky painting.

You can use the picture above as a guide or use something of your own, make it as soft or as dramatic as you want.

I am going to leave you to paint this picture without any guidance from me, you have hopefully enjoyed the exercises so far and I hope that you feel able to use them in this painting.

I would love to see your work, so feel free to send me pictures of your paintings, you never know I may want to use them as examples in my classes.

Technique 8: Masking

For masking your canvas use a good quality decorator's tape, there are a few different brands on the market. These are designed to stop paint bleeding under the tape and will give you crisp clean edges. Using cheap masking tape with lead to disappointing results.

Why use masking?
If you want a straight clean line (lets say a horizon) using a masking tape will give you that crisp edge that you may want.

I use tape if I am painting buildings as I want the building to be crisp and clean against the sky and also keeps the coloured ground clear for when I paint the building its self.

In this unfinished abstract painting I have used masking to get the crisp straight lines of the mast and sails.

I still have work to do, the rigging lines will be added using a rigger brush because using masking tape to paint a very long thin line would be extremely difficult.

For softer edges and irregular shapes you can use cotton wool or torn paper held over the area you want masking, be aware that some types of paper will allow the paint to soak through and onto your canvas.

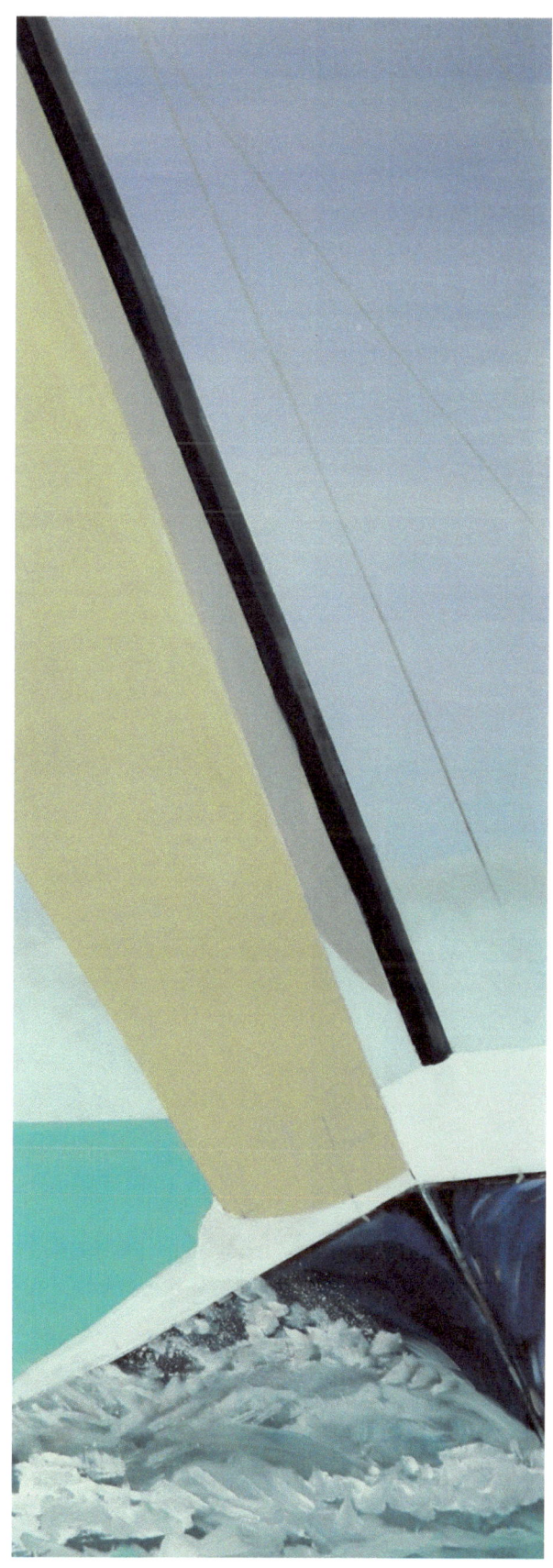

Technique 9: Dry Brushing & Scumbling

Dry brushing is a technique of applying a broken area of colour over a dry layer so that a minimum of paint is applied to the surface letting the other colours show through. The ragged broken look is very expressive and can be used to portray many different features.

It allows you to portray features such as grass, hair or foam on water, other uses are for showing coarse textures such a stone, wood, brickwork, thatch. The list just goes on. Applied over impasto works well to highlight the brushstrokes.

There are Brushes that you can purchase for painting effects such as grass called Rake brushes, others are shaped as a fan, I mostly use bristle brushes for this technique as they have the stiffness that I want to allow me to push the brush around the canvas.

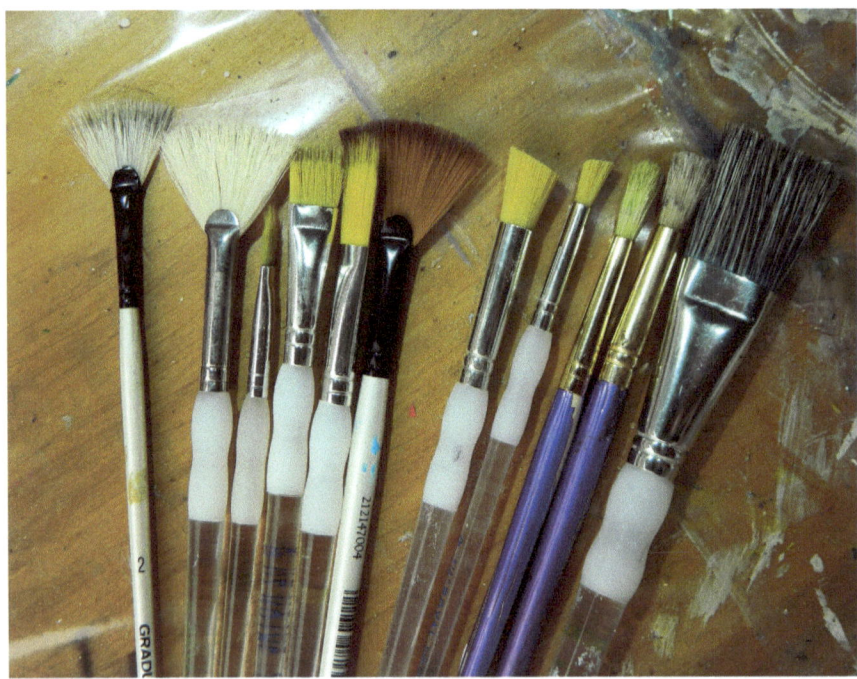

From the left:
Bristle Fan brushes
Rake Brushes
Fan blender
Stippling Brushes
Bristle brushes

Using a minimum of paint on your brush, work quickly and with confidence, don't over work the paint or you will destroy the effect.

Scumbling, is a way of applying a colour over a base colour to achieve an uneven layer. Very much like dry brushing. It can achieve some very attractive effects, used to paint a stone wall or clouds in a sky, Scumbling is a technique you probably have used before and not realised it.

Scumbling can be done using washes of colour overlaying a base colour to produce a hazy effect. I like to lay a wash and using kitchen towel scrub off some of the colour, using additional layers can produce some wonderful mist effects.

You can scumble with glazes, washes or with paint from the tube, do be aware that the purpose of this effect is to let the base colours show through, too much colour will obscure the base layer. I this happens mist the paint with some water and grab the kitchen towel.

So lets have a go.

Exercise 8: Dry Stone wall

Lets try painting a stone wall.

Draw an old stone wall onto your practice paper.
I scumbled the sky, of Light blue painted direct onto the white canvas then with a piece of kitchen towel. I removed areas of blue to give a light cloudy sky.

Old stonework takes on a grey green shade due to moss and other small plant life that like the stone surface. So for the under tone I used a with a grey green mid tone.

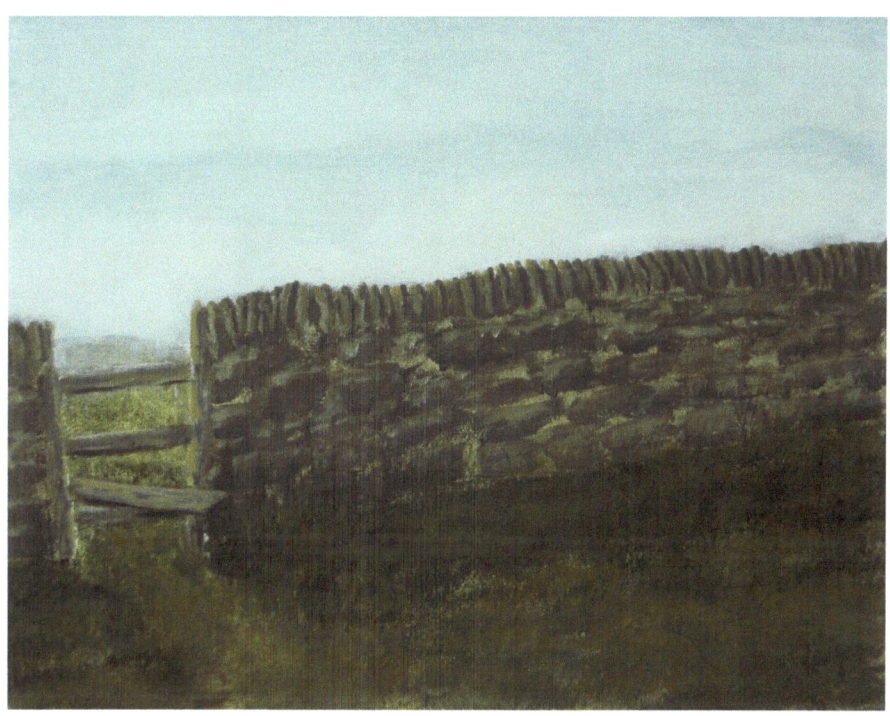

The mid tone can be darkened or lightened to give the range of colour that the stone reflects. Using a little of the colour lightly dab the paint onto the surface to produce the effect of stonework, working with the range of tints you can build up the stonework leaving the mid tone of the under layer showing through.

Finally I used Yellow Ochre with white to make highlights on the wall.

Using Fan brushes to paint the grasses I quickly finished off the picture, well not completely we need more colour in the foreground and perhaps in the background, which I will deal with later on

Technique 10: Sponges

Natural sponge can give some very good effects, I find them especially good at foliage, clouds, mist and fog.

Natural sponge can be purchased from your art shop, usually in a bag containing several pieces of different shapes and sizes. You can also use kitchen sponge or the one you use to wash the car with, cut into shapes and used as stamps these can make some exciting effects for you to paint with.

If you want to add some mist, steam or smoke onto your picture, a sponge with a white glaze can produce the desired effect for you.

Again as I always say, play about with them try different sponges and shapes there are no rules as to what you can and cannot do.

Let's do another exercise.

Exercise 9: Foliage

Landscapes always have some sort of foliage, painting individual leaves may be what you need to do for foreground trees and bushes. But for more background objects using a sponge makes quick work of producing them.

So let's paint a tree.

Start with a blank piece of practice paper and roughly draw a shape of a tree and paint in the trunk and major branches, don't forget that trees are not just brown.

Add shadow detail and highlights where you think they need to be.

Use shades of green greys for moss that may be growing on your tree trunk.

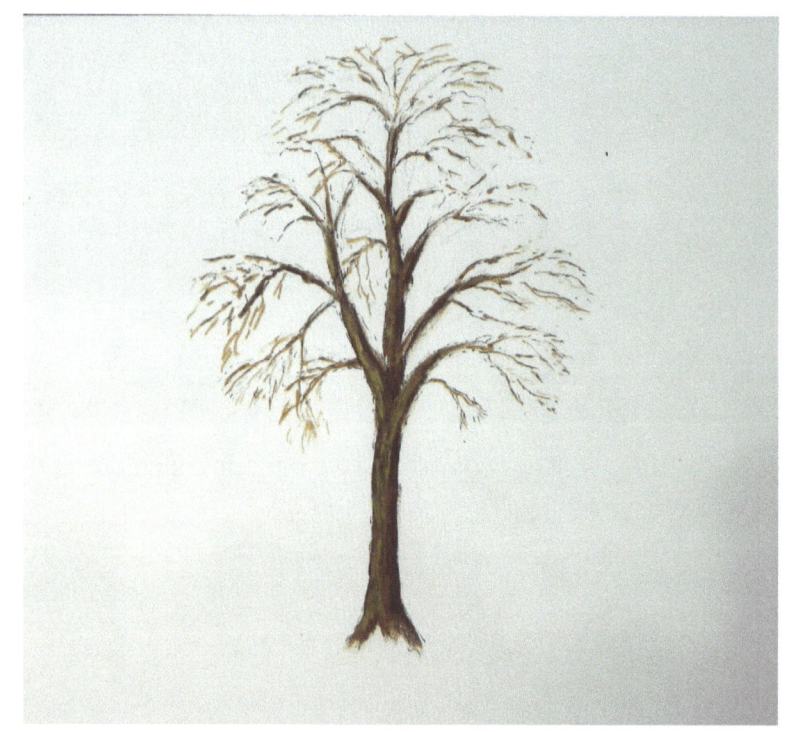

Once the paint is dry we can mix some greens and star adding foliage.

Mixing greens from Ultramarine and Raw Sienna, Yellow Ochre and Cadmium Yellow. You can put in the foliage, start with the darkest green and add the lighter colours on top to show the sunlit foliage, finish off with Cadmium Yellow on its own.

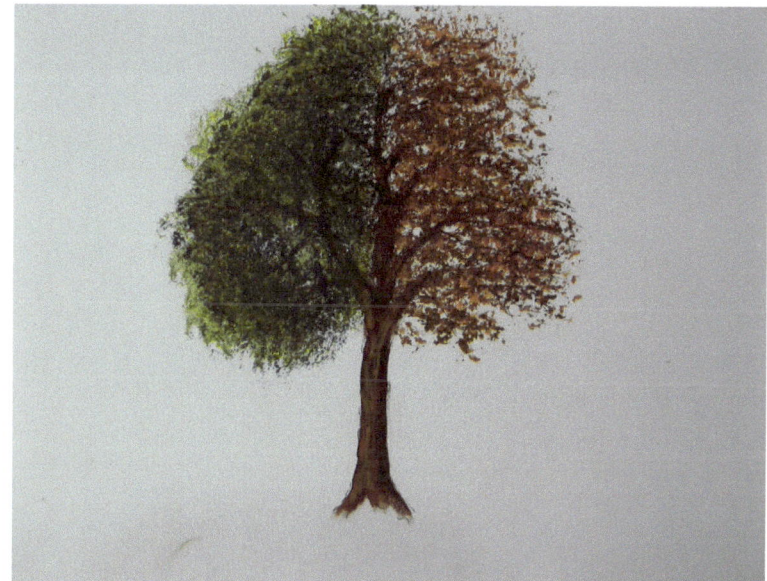

The other side I decided it was autumn. So using Raw Umber, Yellow Ochre, Orange and Cadmium Yellow, mix some golden colours.

Again start with the darkest colour and build up to the lightest.

If you wish try adding some bushes and grass around your tree. If you wish you could add a tree to the picture you made in the previous exercise.

Here is an example of using sponges for painting foliage

Laxey Glenn by Geoff Lewis

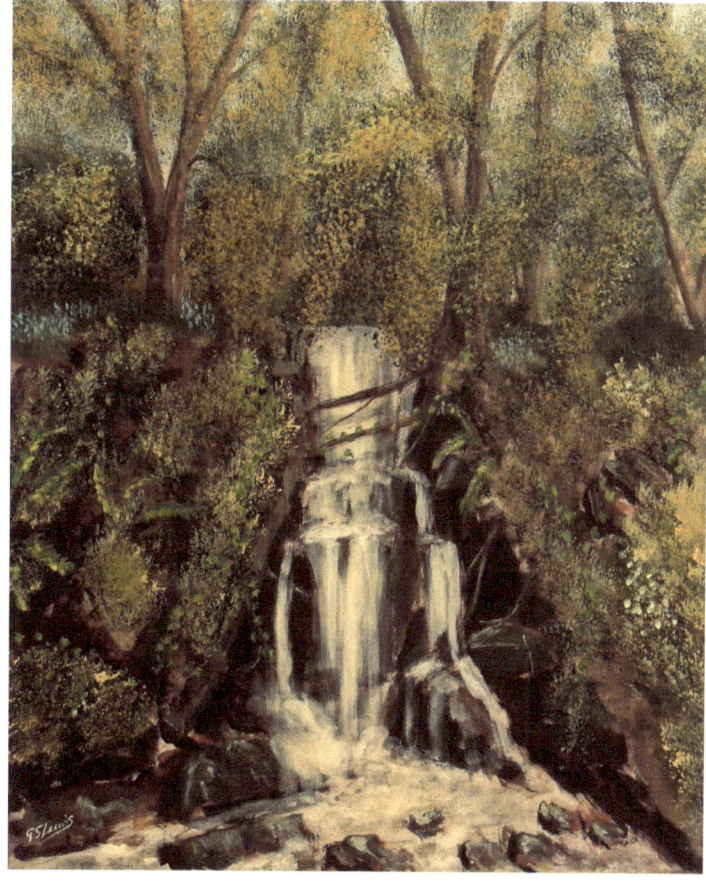

Technique 10: Splattering

Splattering is a way of adding texture to your painting, it can be used to depict leaves on a tree, sea spray, pebbles on a beach.

You can use this technique to add detail to a foreground because of the random patterns you can achieve you can suggest all manner of subjects without over powering your picture.

Or if you fancy yourself as an aspiring Jackson Pollock, splattering can be the object of the painting.

Be aware that paint will travel, so take care to mask areas of the picture that you wish to keep clean.

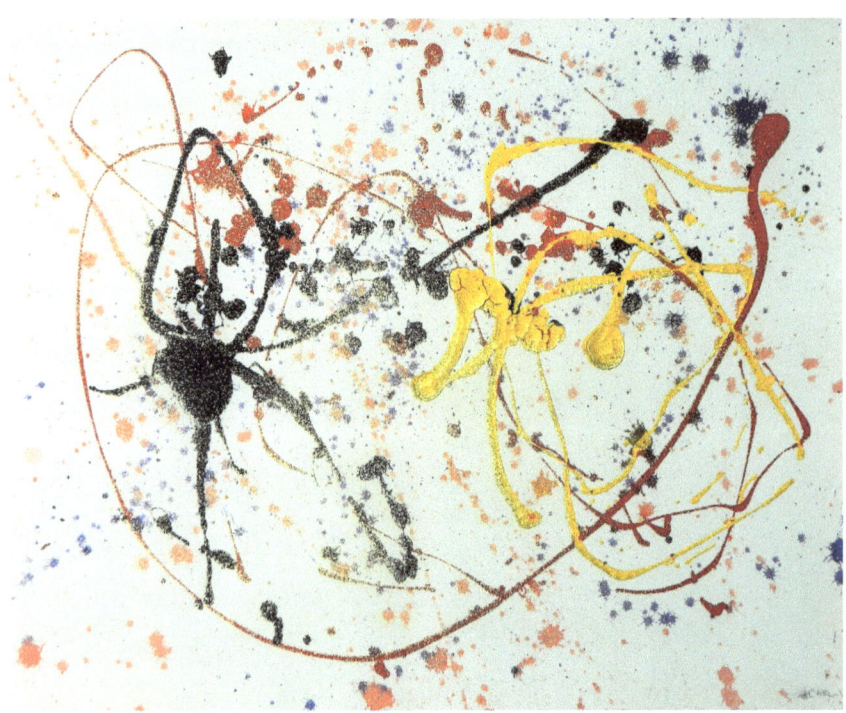

Animals by Mitchell Rose

Most importantly don't use this technique if you have finished paintings in your work area or other material around that could get ruined. My mobile phone cover has a very attractive look with all sorts of colour and shapes splashed on it. Don't forget yourself as it is best you wear something that you don't mind getting messy.

Exercise 10. Splattering

Let's use the picture of the stone wall. I said at the end of that exercise the picture needed more colour so we are going to add some meadow flowers to the foreground.

Firstly we need to mask the upper part of the picture. We could use masking tape and paper, but the hard edge would not look natural, so I will use torn paper.

You could use cotton wool or fabric as long as it is thick enough to not let the paint get to were you don't want it.

Just masking the path and upper part of the wall and using a Bristle fan brush to flick the paint on the picture.

I splattered some orange, yellow and white, which has made a nice effect of meadow flowers.

I will stop at this point but you can carry on if you wish to add more; perhaps a gravel path or some distant trees.

For other effects, try using a comb, or toothbrush (make sure its an old one). For larger areas I have used a gentlemen's hair brush to produce a fine mist of paint also a stiff dustpan brush. Be sure to ask permission first and make sure you clean up thoroughly afterwards.

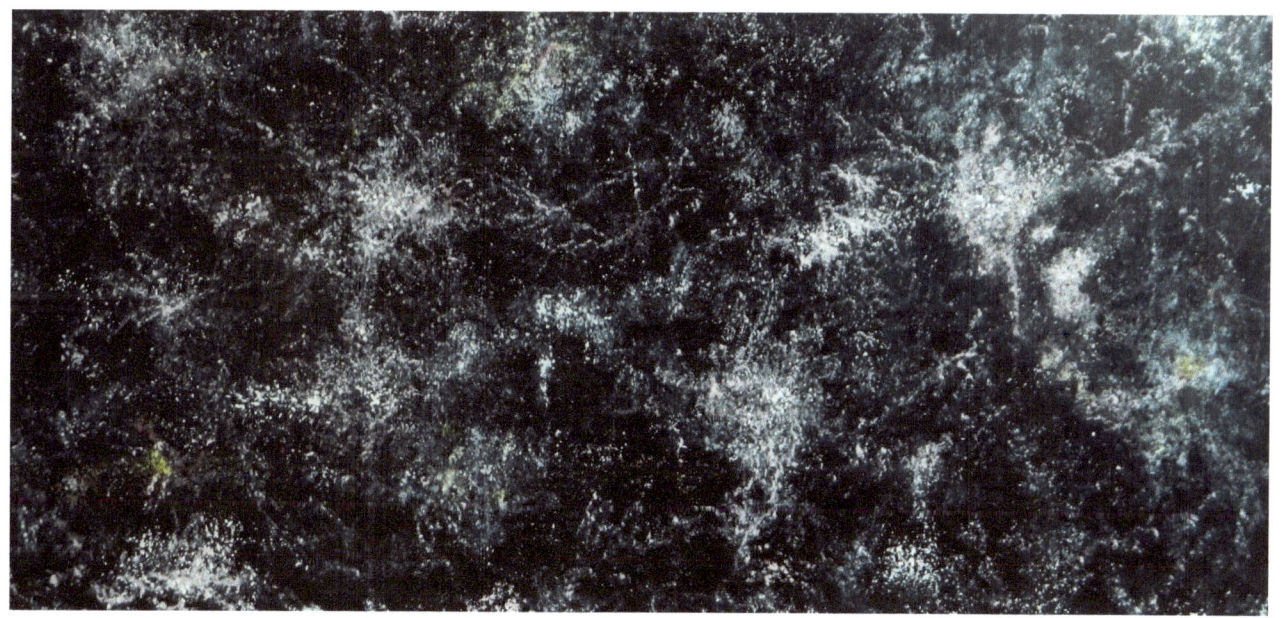

Space by Vaughan Cartwright

This is a large canvas initially painted black then over a period of time the picture has been built up. Can you find the face?

Now that you have started working with acrylic paints, I hope that you continue with the medium as there are many more ways of working with acrylics to explore and enjoy.

I hope that you have enjoyed working through this book.
I am always interested in how my students have got on and I welcome you to contact me to show your work.

art@big-geoff.co.uk

Acknowledgements

I would like to thank the following for their help in making this book possible.

Jules Mariner for keeping me on track.
Vaughan Cartwright, Fiona Henderson,
Linda Caldicott and Mitchell Rose for their kind
permission to use their paintings in this book.

2016 copyright of Geoff lewis

Back cover, Hot stuff by Fiona Henderson

www.ingramcontent.com/pod-product-compliance
Lightning Source LLC
Chambersburg PA
CBHW050841180526
45159CB00004B/1988